the Year of Cozy

125 RECIPES, CRAFTS, AND OTHER *homemade* ADVENTURES

ADRIANNA ADARME

Creator of *A Cozy Kitchen*

RODALE

Rodale books may be purchased for business or promotional use or for special sales. For information, please write to: Special Markets Department, Rodale Inc., 733 Third Avenue, New York, NY 10017

Printed in the United States of America

Rodale Inc. makes every effort to use acid-free ♾, recycled paper ♻.

Hand lettering by Casey Ligon

The photographs on the following pages are by Cynthia Perez: viii, 2, 14, 36, 80, 133, 176, 185, 186–187, 235, and 240.

The photographs on the following pages are by Billy Green: xi (top), 6, 11, 13, 24, 40, 64, 68, 88, 96, 100, 106, 113 (bottom), 118, 119, 120, 123, 130 (bottom), 135, 149 (bottom), 158, 175 (bottom), 178, 179 (bottom), 184, 199, 210, 221, 226 (bottom), and 233.

The images on the following pages are by Flass 100/Shutterstock: xiii–1, 54–55, 124–125, 188–189.

The photographs on page 260 were taken by the following people: (1st row) Whitney Adams, Adrianna Adarme, Adrianna Adarme; (2nd row) Jim Levine, Eugene Yates; (3rd row) Will Thomas, Lucy Quintanilla, Jeff Bercovici.

All other photography is by Adrianna Adarme.

Book design by Rae Ann Spitzenberger

Library of Congress Cataloging-in-Publication Data is on file with the publisher.

ISBN 978–1–62336–510–3 trade hardcover

Distributed to the trade by Macmillan

8   10   9   hardcover

🌿RODALE.

We inspire and enable people to improve their lives and the world around them.
rodalebooks.com

To where home is, Joshua.

*And Amelia, for
making life so messy
and silly and fun.*

*"If I told you that a flower bloomed
in a dark room, would you trust it?"*

—KENDRICK LAMAR

CONTENTS

INTRODUCTION

When I graduated from college, I was, at first, frustrated with my everyday life. There was the Los Angeles traffic that clogged the roads, the lines in the grocery stores, and the perpetual question "What am I doing with my life?" that seemed to fill my thoughts. I couldn't see past the things that irritated me. On a whim, my friend Brendan sent me an e-mail linking me to David Foster Wallace's very famous commencement speech at Kenyon College, "This Is Water." When Wallace told the audience, "Learning how to think really means learning how to exercise some control over how and what you think. It means being conscious and aware enough to choose what you pay attention to and to choose how you construct meaning from experience," it felt as if he was speaking directly to me. I took his words seriously. I may sound a little melodramatic when I say this, but his speech changed the way I live in my day-to-day life. From that moment on, I was committed to choosing my thoughts and actions carefully. I was dedicated to the idea of living my everyday life with intention.

At the time, I couldn't necessarily control every aspect of my life that made me unsatisfied. My job, which left much to be desired, was irreplaceable at the time; we were in the midst of an economic recession, and a big part of me was grateful to simply have a job! And my heart was in pieces after a bad breakup. I felt like I didn't have much to work with, but like Wallace told me, I did have my thoughts, my health, and, most importantly, my free time. So I started there. It was no surprise to my friends when cooking and making things became my "happy place." My blog, *A Cozy Kitchen,* was born out of my desire to share my newfangled hobbies, both of which made my life feel fuller and happier.

I don't think living a good life has to mean fancy things. Sometimes the Internet and books can make us feel like we lack the essence of a sumptuous life. Pictures can appear a bit too perfect; food looks too good to eat—and that's not what I'm after. To me, living a rich life means focusing on the minutiae, the seemingly small, insignificant moments that can pass us by if we don't watch carefully. They're the quiet, chilly morning walks with my corgi, Amelia; the adventure of going on a bike ride in a new part of town; cooking a dinner alongside my boyfriend, Joshua; or even the simple activity of crimping a piecrust. These moments don't require much, just a little planning and intention.

When I set out on the journey to write this book, I felt as if, for the first time in my life, I was in a happy and secure place. I got a book deal! I own a corgi! What else could I want from life? But then, out of the blue, a few of my loved ones began going through

some very difficult times. I found myself worried, sleepless, and a bit hopeless. My heart hurt and twisted in ways it hadn't before. There wasn't much I could do. It made me realize that my life will never be fully "figured out." Life will always throw things at me when I least expect it, and perhaps what I need are coping mechanisms: things that I know will make me happy no matter what. So I began cooking and crafting, except this time it was for this book—this one, the one you're holding!

And yet again, I was losing myself in making a Burnt Cherry and Vanilla Pie (page 167) and carefully arranging a Holiday Wreath (page 38) in the middle of the summer, and it all made me feel oddly accomplished and happy(?). Yes, happy! My problems did not go away, but there was something comforting about losing myself for a few hours in gathering a pile of ingredients, following a few directions, and ending up with something glorious and delicious.

What was it about creating that made me feel better? There's something about making and doing that gives me comfort, and the colder months in fall and winter soothe me most of all. This is why you'll find the book to be organized starting with my favorite month, my birthday month, Amelia's birthday month, October.

I'm not a psychologist, or a social sciences researcher like Brené Brown, PhD, research professor at the University of Houston Graduate College of Social Work (love her). I'm just a woman who found a glimmer of hope and happiness in owning a dog, crafting a trivet, making biscuits, and eating cassoulet. My hope is that this book will inspire you to march into your kitchen or whip out your glue gun and try something new, and then to cozy up—with a warm blanket and cocoa in hand—to the thing you just created. And hopefully a few of your favorite people who make you laugh will be around, too. Because if there's one thing I've learned, it's that the "good life" is measured in moments like these.

Autumn

OCTOBER

GO ON A FALL PICNIC

Autumn is my absolute favorite time to be outside. There's little to no sweating, and mosquitoes aren't flying around. And the leaves, oh, the leaves! Autumn is, hands down, the best season to pack up some lunch and sit on a blanket in nature. I don't like to make it too much of a production. In order to cut the work down, I embrace the idea of half store-bought, half homemade. This means I buy cheeses, charcuterie, bread, and wine but make a fall salad and dessert at home.

My favorite fall salad is as simple as can be. I like to mix a bit of lemon juice and olive oil in a mixing bowl. Then I add a few pinches of salt and pepper. I like to add fresh herbs like Italian parsley and dill, and slices of fall fruit like Fuyu persimmons and/or apples. Pomegranate seeds add some nice color and texture.

My favorite on-the-go dessert is an apple galette. I like to slice up 2 Honeycrisp apples and toss them with 1 teaspoon of cinnamon and ½ cup of brown sugar and a squeeze of lemon juice. I roll out a single piecrust (see page 162), arrange the apples in the center, fold over the edges of the piecrust, brush the dough with an egg wash, and bake at 350°F for 30 minutes, or until golden brown.

GRAIN-FREE DOGGIE DOUGHNUTS

A dog turning a year older should always be an event. You don't have to make it a full-on party (doggie parties can get strange very quickly—trust me, I know), but I do think a small celebration of doughnuts and a candle is fun for the soul. Amelia hates talking about her age, so let's just say she turned 1. Again. **MAKES 1 DOZEN**

2 cups chickpea flour

1 teaspoon baking soda

½ cup natural creamy peanut butter (stir to incorporate any oil on top)

2 tablespoons honey

3 tablespoons melted coconut oil

2 large eggs

½ cup water

1 cup shredded apples (about 2 apples, peeled)

1 Preheat the oven to 325°F. Coat a doughnut pan liberally with cooking spray. In a medium bowl, whisk together the flour and baking soda. Add the peanut butter, honey, oil, eggs, and water. Mix until completely combined and then fold in the shredded apples.

2 Divide half the dough among the 6 cavities in the doughnut pan. Transfer to the oven to bake for 10 to 12 minutes, or until the doughnuts are lightly golden brown and spring back when touched.

3 To remove from the pan, run a butter knife along the inside and outside edges of the doughnuts. Place a wire rack on top of the doughnuts and flip it over, inverting the doughnuts. Repeat the process of spraying the pan, filling it up with the remaining batter, and baking it. Doughnuts will keep for 3 to 5 days when stored in an airtight container at room temperature.

Do

HOMEMADE CANDLES

I have a bit of an obsession with candles. I'm not sure when it became en vogue to buy fancy candles, but I jumped on that bandwagon very quickly. I love them all: girly and floral, woodsy, musty, and spicy. And unfortunately for me, I love to burn these pricey candles all the time! So to curtail my expensive candle-buying habit, I figured it might be time I begin making them at home. At this time of year I love candles to smell like pine needles and cinnamon. It's in anticipation of what's to come. Feel free to customize them according to your liking—there's no wrong way to make candles. The ratios below will give you something that smells like the air a few days before Christmas. If you like, double the batch and have them ready for those last-minute gifts that often come in handy this time of year. MAKES 4

SUPPLIES

4 candlewicks

4 (½-cup) vessels of choice (glass jars or ceramic pots)

8 skewers

1½ cups soy wax or beeswax pellets

Candle-making pot or double boiler

1 tablespoon cedarwood essential oil

4 drops lime essential oil

Tip: All of these candle-making supplies can be found at a craft store and online. The essential oils are easy to find at Whole Foods or other health food stores.

1 To start, set 1 wick in the center of each of the vessels.

2 Rest the skewers closely on both sides of the wicks. When we pour in the hot wax, the wicks will want to move around a bit and these skewers will help stabilize them.

3 Add the wax to your candle-making pot or double boiler top. (You can create a makeshift double boiler by placing a stainless steel bowl over a large pot filled with a few inches of water.) Turn the flame to medium.

4 Heat the wax until melted, about 6 to 8 minutes, being sure not to overheat, which will cause cracking in the final product (if this does happen, not to worry—the candle will still smell delicious and work just fine). When the wax is melted, pour in the cedarwood essential oil and lime essential oil. Mix. Give it a whiff and add a bit more if you like. Pour the hot wax into each of the vessels.

5 Allow the wax to cool completely, 2 to 4 hours, before using the candles.

BURNT BUTTER-PEAR-GINGER CRUMBLE

I love when I can feel fall creeping in. The nights become a bit chillier, the sun begins to set a little earlier, and the light takes on a golden quality. This feeling always makes me want to run to my oven to bake. This crumble will warm your house with all of the smells of the season.

*The butter in this crumble is burnt, not browned. Burnt. I learned to burn my butter from my friend and baker, Hourie. She always takes the butter a bit too far, and it pays off in the flavor department. The spice from the fresh ginger and sweetness from the baked pears make you feel all cozy inside. And since I'm a crazy fan of icy and hot combinations, I say this must, **must** be eaten with a scoop of vanilla ice cream.* MAKES 4 TO 6 SERVINGS

FILLING

3–4 baking pears, peeled, cored, and finely chopped (see note)

¼ cup granulated sugar

¼ cup brown sugar

1 tablespoon all-purpose flour

½" knob peeled fresh ginger, finely chopped

1 teaspoon pure vanilla extract

¼ teaspoon salt

CRUMBLE TOPPING

1 cup all-purpose flour

⅓ cup granulated sugar

¼ cup oat flakes

½ cup coarsely chopped walnuts

½ cup unsalted butter, cubed

1   *To make the filling:* Preheat the oven to 350°F. No need to dirty a bowl: In an 8" x 8" baking dish, combine the pears, sugars, flour, ginger, vanilla, and salt. Toss until the pears are thoroughly coated. Set aside.

2   *To make the topping:* In a medium bowl, whisk together the flour, sugar, oat flakes, and walnuts.

3   In a small saucepan set over medium-high heat, add the cubed butter. Brown the butter until it goes from yellow and bubbling to a very, very dark brown color. It might appear burnt (and it is), but not to worry, it'll taste delicious.

4   Pour the burnt butter into the medium bowl that's holding the flour and oat mixture. Using a spoon, stir the mixture until it's clumpy and everything is coated in butter.

5   Pour the crumble atop the filling and spread it out evenly. Transfer to the oven to bake for 35 to 40 minutes, or until the crumble is bubbling and the top is golden brown.

Note: The best pears for baking are Boscs, Bartletts, green or red Anjous, or Forelles. All hold up nicely in the oven.

Vanilla
ice cream
is a must!

MARBLED BOWLS

It's no big secret that I love marble, actual natural marble. The lines and variances of shapes are so beautiful. Last Christmas, I took my obsession with marble into the kitchen when I made a cranberry-marbled cheesecake for my blog. And now, I'm taking it into my craft closet with these marbled bowls. If you're like me and have bottles of nail polish just sitting in your bathroom, then this DIY is perfect for you. This technique of marbling with nail polish can be applied to a variety of vessels like vases, mugs, and ramekins.

A few tips to keep in mind before you start:

- Get everything prepped and then move quickly. The nail polish dries in the water very fast!

- Use hot water. Cold water will make the nail polish seize.

- Pour the nail polish close to the surface of the water. If you pour it from too high a distance, it will bead up and sink to the bottom.

- Pour the 2 nail polishes at the same time.

- If on the first try you don't succeed, don't worry. Remember that nail polish remover is your friend, if you need to start again.

SUPPLIES

Shallow container such as a pie pan (I used a shallow baking dish)

Gray nail polish

Mint green nail polish

Skewer

White bowls (see note)

Craft paper or old newspaper

Note: Do not use any vessel that is unglazed. I used very inexpensive white CorningWare bowls that I purchased from Target in the sale section. These bowls work very well because they are high gloss, which means that the nail polish rubs off very easily with a bit of nail polish remover. I also recommend using white bowls so the nail polish colors pop.

1   Fill the shallow container with hot water.

2   Open the 2 nail polishes and hold them close to the surface of the water. Pour them into the water at the same time.

3   Moving quickly, run the skewer through the center, creating a swirl effect.

4   Dip the sides of a bowl into the water. In order to get swirls all the way around, you'll need to repeat with fresh water and nail polish. If any nail polish has seeped into the center of the bowl, remove it using nail polish remover and a cotton ball. Repeat with the rest of the bowls. Place the bowls on a sheet of craft paper or old newspaper to dry for 5 hours.

5   Once the bowls are completely dry, remove any excess nail polish on the bottoms of the bowls or around the rim. Wash the insides of the bowls thoroughly with soap and water. These bowls are food safe (as long as there is no nail polish inside them) and should be strictly hand-washed.

Tip: The container that held the water and nail polish mixture will have some bits of nail polish on the sides and the bottom. I removed the nail polish with a cotton ball and nail polish remover and washed the container thoroughly with hot water and soap.

PEANUT BUTTER CUPS

*Amelia is my spirit animal. We are sometimes cranky and bossy, usually lovable, optimistic at the core, and we both love, **love** peanut butter. There have been moments when she and I have lain in bed together eating apple slices dipped in peanut butter. They weren't our highest moments, but it happened and we've moved on. When it comes to Halloween, Amelia and I are lukewarm about the holiday. The spooky decor actually scares me, and Amelia always feels objectified when I dress her up in embarrassing costumes, though I still do it because, well, she's just too entertaining for me not to. The one redeeming thing about the holiday is homemade candy. And it should come as no surprise that my ultimate favorite is homemade peanut butter cups.* MAKES 9

½ cup unsalted or salted creamy peanut butter

2 tablespoons confectioners' sugar

Sea salt

1 cup cocoa powder

½ cup coconut oil, melted and warm

⅓ cup maple syrup

1½ teaspoons vanilla extract

Note: I recommend using natural peanut butter because the flavor is far superior and it contains no sugar. Just be sure to give it a good stir so the oil that resides on the top is reincorporated.

1   Place liners into 9 muffin cups. In a small bowl, add the peanut butter and the confectioners' sugar. Using a hand mixer with the whisk attachment, beat until light, fluffy, and completely combined. If using unsalted peanut butter, add a few pinches of sea salt to taste (I like Maldon).

2   In a medium bowl, combine the cocoa powder, coconut oil, maple syrup, and vanilla extract. Stir until very smooth.

3   Spoon 1 tablespoon of chocolate mixture into each liner. Smack the muffin tin on the counter to even out the chocolate. Transfer to the freezer for 5 minutes, or until the chocolate is firm.

4   Remove the muffin tin from the freezer and add 1 to 2 teaspoons of peanut butter mixture to each cup. Top with 1 to 2 additional tablespoons of chocolate and place in the freezer for 5 to 10 minutes, or until firm. Transfer to the refrigerator to thaw for about 30 minutes. Store in the refrigerator until ready to serve. When it's time to serve, sprinkle a pinch of sea salt atop each peanut butter cup.

Tip: Since this recipe contains no stabilizers for the chocolate, if the peanut butter cups are kept at room temperature for too long, they'll melt, so just be sure to keep them in the refrigerator until serving.

NOVEMBER

HOW TO MAKE NEW FRIENDS (AS AN ADULT)

I cherish my friendships. I value them because for a long time I didn't have a core set of friends. I was a bit of a loner and sort of all over the place. Making new friends, once you get out of college and move to a new city, can be challenging: You aren't forced together with a large group of people your own age anymore like you were in college, and maintaining friendships with full-time jobs and other real-life, grown-up obligations can be tough. Nevertheless, in the past few years I've made some of my closest friends. Here are some things I learned along the way.

1 Start a hobby (see page 241). I guarantee you'll make friends in that environment.

2 Use social media. This may sound a bit strange, but I've met some of my best friends through the Internet. I usually just e-mail people I've been admiring for a long time and ask them to lunch.

3 Ask your guy friends if they know someone you should be friends with. I've been set up on "girl dates" by a few guy friends, and they're usually right!

4 When you meet someone for the first time, share something meaningful. I'm not telling you to divulge your most guarded secrets, family dramas, and every trial and tribulation you've ever endured. But in order to connect, people need to feel like they're getting something real.

5 Don't be a flake and not show up for lunches or dates. Just don't.

Do

PUMPKIN ARRANGEMENT
WITH PERSIMMONS AND COTTON

I like my pumpkins weird. I'm talking about the ones in varying colors, with bumps all over their skins and stems that resemble hooks. Feel free to seek out a fantasy pumpkin (pictured) or use a plain ol' pumpkin! Cotton branches warm up this flower arrangement, giving it a beautiful texture and lightness that I adore. And the persimmons on their branches foreshadow what will be featured on the Thanksgiving table.

SUPPLIES

Pumpkin of choice

1 bunch cotton branches

1 bunch persimmons on their branches

1 bunch baby's breath

1   Using a sharp paring knife, cut a hole out of the top of the pumpkin. (I found that if the hole was too small, the branches couldn't hang to the right or left, so be sure it's big enough.) Discard the top and remove the seeds. (Save them for roasting!)

2   Trim the cotton branches and persimmon branches to your liking and arrange them in the pumpkin. There's no wrong way to do this! I like when their heights are slightly different. Fill in the bare spots with baby's breath. Pour a little water inside the pumpkin and place on a table.

Tip: To roast pumpkin seeds, wash the seeds thoroughly. Preheat the oven to 325°F. In a bowl, drizzle the seeds with olive oil. Toss them with a few pinches of cumin, maybe some curry powder, and salt for a savory flavor, or use cinnamon and sugar for a sweet version. Spread the seeds out on a baking sheet and transfer to the oven to roast for 10 to 15 minutes, or until golden brown. Remove, allow to cool, and eat.

"CHORIZO"-SPICED SQUASH SOUP

There isn't a lick of pork in this soup. Instead, it simply borrows the flavors that are typically found in chorizo sausage. I borrowed this idea from my boyfriend, who, for a month straight, made everything he could get his hands on chorizo spiced: There was grilled octopus, braised chicken, mussels in butter—it was a good month! When the temperatures drop, this soup feels like a warm hug in a bowl. If you make a salad and serve this soup with bread, it instantly becomes dinner, and if you like, you could even thin the soup with more broth, add some Parmesan cheese, and toss it with cooked pasta. It's versatile. And maybe a bit of a show-off.

MAKES 4 SERVINGS

1 acorn squash (2½ pounds), halved, seeds scooped out

2 tablespoons olive oil

1 shallot, finely chopped

1 clove garlic, minced

1 cup canned pumpkin puree

1 teaspoon ancho chile powder

1 teaspoon salt + additional, to taste

½ teaspoon dried oregano

1 teaspoon ground cumin

¼ teaspoon ground coriander

Teeny pinch of ground cloves

3 cups water or vegetable broth

Juice from ½ lemon

1 Preheat the oven to 350°F. Line a baking sheet with parchment paper. Place the squash, cut sides down, on the baking sheet and roast for about 30 minutes, or until mostly tender. Scoop the flesh into a small bowl. There might be some bits of the squash that aren't completely cooked—not to worry, the rest will cook in the pot with the broth.

2 In a medium pot or Dutch oven, heat the oil over medium heat. Add the shallot and cook until softened, about 2 minutes. Add the garlic, cooked squash, pumpkin, chile powder, 1 teaspoon salt, oregano, cumin, coriander, and cloves. Cook for 2 to 3 minutes, or until the spices are fragrant.

(continued)

¼ cup pepitas

1 teaspoon olive oil

¼ teaspoon ancho chile powder

¼ teaspoon ground cumin

Pinch of ground coriander

Salt

3 tablespoons crème fraîche

3 Pour in the water or vegetable broth and lemon juice. Bring to a simmer over medium-high heat and cook for about 10 minutes, or until the squash is completely softened. Using an immersion blender, pulse until smooth, about 30 seconds. (If you don't own one, no biggie—just transfer the soup, in batches, to a blender. Lightly cover the blender with the lid, being sure to allow a bit of air to escape, and puree until smooth.) Return the soup to the pot and set it over low heat to keep it warm. Taste the soup and adjust the salt—I added about an additional 1 teaspoon and it really brought out the flavor from the spices.

4 *To make the soup topping:* In a small skillet over medium heat, add the pepitas, oil, chile powder, cumin, coriander, and pinch of salt. Toss to combine and toast for about 3 minutes, or until the pepitas' edges have turned lightly golden brown. Divide the soup among the bowls and drizzle a bit of crème fraîche on top. Top with the pepitas. Serve with a side of bread.

Make

FLAKY, BUTTERY BISCUITS

Some days I dream about opening a little bakery of my own. The walls would be adorned with cute stuff, while an array of wild plants would hang from the ceilings. The Marzocco machine (making frothy cappuccinos) would hiss and sing, and wafts of yeast, butter, and sweet things would dance through the air. The star would be pie for dessert and biscuits for breakfast. These fluffy domes of butter, pictured on page 22, are—dare I say?—perfect. They're flaky and magical and, like any good biscuit, they're able to play a supporting role in a breakfast sandwich or shine in a basket on a Thanksgiving table. MAKES 8

2 cups all-purpose flour

1 tablespoon baking powder

½ teaspoon baking soda

1 scant teaspoon fine-grain sea salt (table salt works, too!)

¾ cup unsalted butter, frozen

½ cup buttermilk, cold and shaken

1 large egg, cold

EGG WASH
1 large egg
1 tablespoon milk or water

1 **To make the biscuits:** Preheat the oven to 400°F. Line a baking sheet with parchment paper.

2 In a large bowl, mix together the flour, baking powder, baking soda, and salt. Using a box grater, grate the butter into the flour mixture. Gently break up the butter with a fork and toss it in the flour until the butter resembles small peas. Transfer to the freezer to chill for 10 minutes.

3 In a small bowl, whisk the buttermilk and egg until combined.

4 **To make the egg wash:** In another small bowl, whisk together the egg and milk or water. Transfer the egg wash to the refrigerator.

5 Remove the flour mixture from the freezer. Add the buttermilk mixture all at once to the flour mixture. Mix until just combined. Lightly knead the dough in the bowl until it forms a solid mass. Sprinkle your kitchen counter or other work surface with flour and dump the dough onto it. Press the dough into a ¾" thickness. Cut out the biscuits using a 2½" biscuit cutter, ending up with about 6 biscuits. You can recombine the scraps and get 2 more biscuits. Transfer them to the baking sheet.

(continued)

6 Put the biscuits in the freezer to chill for 5 to 7 minutes. After the biscuits are cold, brush the tops with the egg wash and bake for 10 to 12 minutes, or until tall and medium golden brown. Serve the biscuits warm, with honey, jam, or plain ol' butter.

FLOUR

POSE

1 C

23

Do

THANKSGIVING NAME TAGS

These name tags couldn't be simpler, and that's what I love most about them. They can be thrown together in a few minutes or even delegated to a family member in need of a job on Thanksgiving Day. I borrowed some baby's breath from an arrangement I'd already made, but feel free to use any other filler-type flower you may find at the market.

SUPPLIES

Twigs (from a tree outside)
Sprigs fresh rosemary
Baby's breath (Gypsophila)
Twine
Note cards

1 Break the twigs into 3" sticks. Trim the ends with a pair of shears, if you like.

2 Gather about 3 or 4 sticks, 2 sprigs of rosemary, and a few pieces of baby's breath. Tie with a piece of twine and trim.

3 Write names on the note cards and trim the cards appropriately. Stick the cards in between the twigs and rosemary.

Make

NO-BAKE PUMPKIN CHIFFON PIE

*Okay, so I lied. There is **some** baking in this recipe, but only 8 minutes' worth! I'm not lucky enough to have a double oven, and I'm guessing you probably don't have one either, so enter this pie!*

I fell in love with chiffon pies a few years ago; they're wonderfully light, and their texture is silky smooth. Gelatin (versus a large amount of eggs) helps achieve this beautiful texture. For years I strictly made egg-heavy pumpkin pies. I got over it and began the search for something that wouldn't bog you down even more after a large meal. I found a happy medium: fewer eggs and a bit of gelatin. Now, I reserve my oven for other important things like biscuits, stuffing, and turkey, and I use my fridge to make this perfect pumpkin pie. MAKES ONE 9" PIE

CRUST

2 cups gingersnap crumbs (from about 30 cookies)

¼ teaspoon salt

¼ cup unsalted butter, melted

FILLING

3 tablespoons dark rum

2 teaspoons unflavored powdered gelatin

1 cup pumpkin puree

⅓ cup heavy cream

⅓ cup + ¼ cup sugar

2 large eggs, separated

½ teaspoon ground cinnamon

½ teaspoon ground ginger

¼ teaspoon freshly grated nutmeg

¼ teaspoon ground allspice

¼ teaspoon salt

Freshly whipped cream

1 ***To make the crust:*** Preheat the oven to 350°F. Place the crumbs and salt in a medium bowl. Pour in the butter and mix until the gingersnap crumbs are moist. Transfer to a 9" pie dish and press the crumbs firmly and evenly until they line the bottom and sides of the dish. Bake until slightly darker in color and firm to the touch, about 8 to 10 minutes. Allow the crust to cool completely before adding the filling.

2 ***To make the filling:*** Pour the rum into a small bowl. Sprinkle the gelatin atop the rum and set aside.

3 In a medium saucepan set over medium-low heat, add the pumpkin, heavy cream, ⅓ cup sugar, 2 egg yolks, cinnamon, ginger, nutmeg, allspice, and salt. Cook the mixture, stirring, until it reaches a temperature of 175°F. Transfer the pumpkin mixture to a medium bowl and stir in the rum and gelatin. Set aside to cool.

(continued)

4 Meanwhile, in the metal bowl of a stand mixer, beat the 2 egg whites until they begin to hold peaks. With the beaters still going, sprinkle in the remaining ¼ cup sugar and continue beating until stiff peaks form.

5 Gently fold the egg whites into the cooled pumpkin mixture. Add the pie filling to the gingersnap pie shell and transfer to the fridge to set for 5 hours. Serve with a topping of freshly whipped cream and garnish with gingersnap cookie crumbs or a dusting of ground cinnamon.

Shopping Tip: You can usually find gelatin right next to the Jell-O in your grocery store. It comes in two forms: powder and sheets. I use the powder, but either would work for this recipe. If you do buy the sheets, you'll need 2 for this recipe.

Note: Whenever I fold whipped raw egg whites into a dessert, I make sure to use good-quality organic eggs.

Live

GIVE SOMEONE DINNER IN A BOX

I'm guessing there's a person in your life who never thinks too much about himself or herself. This person is most likely overworked, always exhausted, and in need of a gigantic hug. And probably also hungry. This person deserves Dinner in a Box. To give the joyous gift of dinner, here's what to include.

1 Baguette

2 Red wine

3 Store-bought dried pasta

4 A jar of good-quality marinara sauce

5 A chunk of Parmesan cheese

6 A jar of red-pepper flakes

7 Pot of basil

8 And a card that says "Happy Holidays!" or "You're special."

DECEMBER

Do

HOMEMADE WRAPPING PAPER

Making homemade wrapping paper might be one of my favorite holiday crafts. Sure, you can easily buy wrapping paper, and I do that, too, but if I can, I definitely go the homemade route because this means that my personality really gets to shine when I hand my friends and family gifts. I enlist three different tools to help me achieve super-easy homemade wrapping paper: a spray bottle, a stamp, and a paintbrush.

SUPPLIES

1 roll of brown or white craft paper

Spray bottle

1 small bottle of acrylic paint, color of choice

Stamp of choice (I chose a Christmas tree stamp)

Ink pad

Watercolor palette

1 paintbrush

1   Begin by cutting your pieces of brown or white craft paper into the sizes you need to wrap your presents. If you haven't purchased your presents yet, feel free to cut large sheets of both so they're ready to go when you're ready to wrap.

2   *Spray bottle method:* Fill your spray bottle with water and drop in about a tablespoon (you can eyeball this measurement) of paint. Replace the spray attachment and shake vigorously until the water and paint are thoroughly combined. Hold the spray bottle about 6 inches away from the sheet of paper and spray all over, being sure to leave some negative space. Allow the paint to dry for 15 minutes before wrapping your package.

3   *Stamping method:* You know how to do this! Press your stamp of choice onto the ink pad and stamp away. I like to do a pattern of sorts: one row of trees facing one way and then another row of trees facing the opposite way. Allow the ink to dry for 30 minutes before wrapping your package.

4   *Watercolor method:* Choose the colors you like beforehand. Feel free to brush the colors you'll be using next to one another on a scrap piece of paper. I chose to do a line pattern, alternating colors and then flipping the pattern in the other direction with the next box. Repeat this until the entire sheet of wrapping paper is filled. Allow the paint to dry for 30 minutes before wrapping your package.

GOLDEN MILK TEA, WARM CHAI TEA, AND DECADENT HOT CHOCOLATE

When I was a kid, I would sit in front of the television, drinking hot Swiss Miss and dunking— wait for it—slices of white bread into my cup. Yes, it was like hot cocoa bread, which sounds sort of gross at first when I think about it, but also sort of delicious. While my childhood was all about hot chocolate, college was the time for the more grown-up warm chai. Before, during, and after class, there was always something about the spice, caffeine, and sweetness that clicked with my always-working brain. Now, I love golden milk tea in the afternoon. It makes me feel like I'm on a health kick without exploring any of those crazy juice cleanses that would, frankly, just make the people around me suffer because hanger—anger meets hunger—is real, duh.

Each of these drinks is vastly different. If you've never had fresh turmeric steeped in almond milk, you're in for a treat. Turmeric's anti-inflammatory properties are good for when you're feeling under the weather. The warm chai tea is on the spicier side of spicy, so if you like, feel free to decrease the ginger knob to 3 inches. And the hot chocolate is decadent, spicy, and luxurious . . . just like you.

Golden Milk Tea

Warm Chai Tea

Decadent Hot Chocolate

GOLDEN MILK TEA

MAKES 4 SERVINGS

2 cups almond milk

3 tablespoons good-quality honey

3" knob peeled fresh turmeric

1" knob peeled fresh ginger

1   In a medium saucepan over medium heat, pour in the almond milk and honey. Using a zester, grate the turmeric and fresh ginger into the mixture.

2   Heat until very warm. Turn off the heat, cover the pot, and allow the milk tea to steep for 2 to 3 minutes.

3   Strain the mixture and divide among 4 mugs.

WARM CHAI TEA

MAKES 4 SERVINGS

2 teaspoons black peppercorns (about 20 peppercorns)

10 whole cloves

6 pods cardamom

4" knob peeled fresh ginger, cut into rounds

2 sticks cinnamon

6 cups cold water

6 bags black tea

2 cups whole milk or almond milk

½ cup sugar

1   On a cutting board, using the back of a chef's knife, crush the black peppercorns, cloves, and cardamom pods. Place them in a medium saucepan over medium heat. Add the ginger and cinnamon sticks and toast for 2 to 3 minutes, or until fragrant.

2   Add the water and bring to a boil over medium-high heat, then reduce the heat to medium-low and simmer for 10 minutes.

3   Add the tea bags, turn off the heat, and cover the pot so the tea can steep for 5 minutes.

4   Discard the tea bags and pour in the milk and sugar. Stir until the sugar dissolves. Reheat the tea, if needed, over medium heat. Pour the tea through a strainer into 4 mugs.

DECADENT HOT CHOCOLATE

MAKES 4 SERVINGS

4 cups whole milk or coconut milk

2 tablespoons sugar

1 stick cinnamon

¼ vanilla bean, scraped, or 2 teaspoons pure vanilla extract

6 ounces dark chocolate (60% cacao content)

¼ teaspoon ancho chile powder

Pinch of salt

Marshmallows (optional— see page 182 to make your own)

1 In a medium saucepan over low heat, add the milk, sugar, cinnamon stick, and vanilla bean scrapings (called caviar) and pod or vanilla extract. Heat to a very gentle simmer, then take the saucepan off the heat and allow the liquid to steep for 10 to 15 minutes. Remove the cinnamon stick and vanilla bean pod and discard.

2 Meanwhile, create a double boiler by setting a stainless steel or glass bowl over a saucepan filled with simmering water. Add the chocolate to the bowl and heat until the chocolate is melted.

3 Place the saucepan with the steeped milk over medium-low heat and pour in the melted chocolate. Whisk until completely incorporated and hot.

4 Add the chile powder and a pinch of salt. Divide among 4 mugs and top with marshmallows, if desired.

GO FORAGING

I'm not gonna lie, when my boyfriend first told me he was gonna go foraging in our neighborhood, I sort of rolled my eyes, laughed a little, and called him a hipster. (And yes, I realize I'm wearing that hat.) My tune changed when he returned with a bag full of bright greens and edible flowers. Wait, you mean I didn't have to pay for this stuff? I'll admit that that is definitely part of what hooked me. The next time he went, I followed. He pointed out sorrel and its flowers growing so abundantly right by the road, a frond of fennel growing between the cracks of the sidewalk; it felt just like treasure hunting.

Foraging will depend on your region and what's growing around you. In California, especially during the rainier months, look for sorrel, wood sorrel, radish pods, fennel fronds, and nasturtium (pictured). Each has a different flavor profile; for example, sorrel is tart and fragrant, while nasturtium is a bit spicy. And all of them also have flowers that are even more flavorful than their leaf counterparts. If you're interested in what grows in your area, do some Googling; you might be able to find a foraging class in your area. Or you could go to the library and check out a book specific to your region that points out what wild plants and flowers you should look for.

Soon your neighborhood walks will be like a trip to the grocery store. Nothing makes me happier than going on my walks with Amelia only to come home with a fistful of ingredients for dinner, like the Nasturtium Bucatini on page 144.

Do

MAKE A HOLIDAY WREATH

It took me years to finally start buying Christmas decorations. Most of the time, I wasn't sure what the point was since I usually fly home to my parents' house. But then, I craved being around pretty lights and ornaments, so I began buying them little by little. Now, nothing thrills me more than pulling out my box of Christmas decorations the day after Thanksgiving. I lo-o-o-o-ve making my own holiday wreath. They've varied in theme over the years, with some more elaborate than others, but my all-time favorites are simple and have a Donald Trump– type comb-over with beautiful adornments like cute little kumquats or, in this case, pretty rose hip berries.

SUPPLIES

10–12 bay laurel branches

1 (12" or 14") grapevine wreath

Branch clippers or strong floral clippers

Floral wire

10 rose hip branches with berries attached

Filler greenery (see note)

2 pomegranates, 1 halved

6 (3") floral picks

1 ribbon or thick twine or wreath hook

Note: I suggest 5 or 6 bunches of any standard green leafy filler, like eucalyptus, Israeli ruscus, or citrus leaves.

1 Start by laying everything side by side. Begin with the bay laurel. Nestle the bay laurel branches within the grapevine, trimming the ends, if needed, with the clippers. Go in one direction, from the bottom left side, all the way around to the top. There is no right way with arranging! Step back from time to time to see how everything is looking. Adjust as you see fit. Tie each branch of laurel to the grapevine using a small piece of floral wire.

2 Add the rose hip branches, spacing them however you like, attaching them with the floral wire when needed. (These branches are on the heavier side, so all of mine needed to be attached.) Hold up the wreath and give it a look. You may need to add more laurel or rose hip branches. Next, add the filler greenery in any spots that you feel need it. Finally, score the backs of the halved pomegranate with 2 floral picks each and, using floral wire, tie the floral picks to the grapevine. Repeat with the remaining whole pomegranate. Place them where you see fit. I chose to place 2 together toward the bottom and 1 higher up on the wreath.

(continued)

Tip: Rose hip, bay laurel, and citrus branches are usually sold at flower markets or farmers' markets. Most larger cities have them. If you can't find rose hip branches, no biggie! Replace them with holly berries, coffee bean branches, or kumquat branches.

3 To hang, you can add a wreath hook on the back, or you can simply thread a sturdy piece of thick twine or ribbon through the back of the grapevine. Make sure it's secure! The pomegranates make this wreath on the heavier side. If you're using the ribbon or twine, secure with a thumbtack or nail to the very top of your door (the part that slides into the door frame) so that there is no visible hole. Then let the wreath hang down against your door.

HOLIDAY COOKIES GALORE

If Thanksgiving is a pie holiday, then Christmas is all about cookies. Cookies galore. I'm going to be honest: I'm much more of a pie girl than a cookie girl. And good cake probably comes even before cookies. But a well-baked cake is hard to come by, so I guess you can say I like cookies, especially when they're warm and dunked in milk.

These three holiday cookies are all very different and yield varied textures and flavors. The Chewy Chai Snickerdoodles are, well, delightfully chewy, with the right amount of spice. The Dark Chocolate Chunk Turtle Cookies are stout in posture and full of fun stuff like pecans, melty caramel, and gooey chocolate. The Rye Walnut Lace Cookies are wispy thin, crispy around the edges, and chewy in the center. The drizzle of icing makes them appear winter wonderland–esque. All are delicious, and each has the one ingredient every cookie needs: a good amount of salt.

(continued)

Chewy Chai
Snickerdoodles

Rye Walnut
Lace Cookies

Dark Chocolate
Chunk Turtle Cookies

CHEWY CHAI SNICKERDOODLES

MAKES 18
SNICKERDOODLES

2¼ cups all-purpose flour

1 teaspoon baking powder

½ teaspoon baking soda

½ teaspoon fine-grain
sea salt

1 teaspoon ground ginger

½ teaspoon ground
cinnamon

¼ teaspoon ground
cardamom

¼ teaspoon ground cloves

¼ teaspoon ground allspice

¼ teaspoon freshly ground
black pepper

1½ cups sugar

2 ounces cream cheese,
at room temperature

6 tablespoons unsalted
butter, melted and slightly
cooled

⅓ cup vegetable oil

1 large egg

2 tablespoons milk

1 teaspoon pure vanilla
extract

SUGAR AND SPICE
COATING

¼ cup sugar

1 teaspoon ground
cinnamon

Pinch of ground cardamom

1 **To make the snickerdoodles:** Preheat the oven to 350°F. Line 2 baking sheets with parchment paper.

2 In a medium bowl, whisk together the flour, baking powder, baking soda, salt, ginger, cinnamon, cardamom, cloves, allspice, and pepper.

3 To the large bowl of a stand mixer, add the sugar, cream cheese, and butter. Beat until light and fluffy, about 1 minute. Add the oil and beat until incorporated. Next, add the egg, milk, and vanilla. Continue to beat until smooth. In 2 additions, add the flour mixture, being sure to scrape down the sides of the bowl in between, until just mixed. The dough will be soft. Rest on the counter for 15 minutes while you preheat the oven.

4 **To make the coating:** On a small plate, mix together the sugar, cinnamon, and cardamom. Divide the dough into 18 equal pieces of about 2 tablespoons each. Using your hands, roll the dough pieces into balls. Working in batches, roll the balls in the sugar and spice mixture and evenly space about 6 dough balls on each baking sheet. Sprinkle the tops evenly with some of the remaining sugar and spice mixture.

5 Bake 1 tray at a time for 11 to 12 minutes, rotating the tray after 7 minutes, or until the edges are set and just beginning to brown. Continue until all the cookies are baked. Let the cookies cool on the baking sheets for 5 minutes. Transfer the cookies to a wire rack and let cool to room temperature before serving.

DARK CHOCOLATE CHUNK TURTLE COOKIES

MAKES 22 COOKIES

2⅔ cups all-purpose flour

1 cup whole wheat flour

1½ teaspoons baking powder

1¼ teaspoons baking soda

1 teaspoon fine-grain
sea salt

1¼ cups unsalted butter,
softened

1¼ cups light or dark brown
sugar

1 cup granulated sugar

2 large eggs

1 teaspoon pure vanilla
extract

12 ounces dark chocolate
chunks (at least 69% cacao
content)

½ cup chopped pecans

12 store-bought caramels,
diced (about ½ cup)

Sea salt, for garnish
(I like Maldon)

1 In a large bowl, mix together the flours, baking powder, baking soda, and salt.

2 In the bowl of a stand mixer, using the paddle attachment, beat the butter and sugars together until the mixture turns a pale brown color, about 2 to 3 minutes. Crack in the eggs and pour in the vanilla. Beat once more until the eggs are fully incorporated. In 2 batches, add the flour mixture, beating just until the flour is fully incorporated. Pour in the dark chocolate chunks and pecans.

3 Transfer the dough to the refrigerator for at least 8 hours or, ideally, overnight.

4 Preheat the oven to 350°F. Line 2 baking sheets with parchment paper. Using a #40 cookie scoop or 2 tablespoons, scoop out balls of dough and place them about 3" apart on the baking sheets. Push a few pieces of caramel into the tops of each mound of cookie dough. Push in the tops of the cookies slightly with your hands and sprinkle with a pinch of sea salt. Bake one baking sheet at a time for 12 to 15 minutes, or until the edges are lightly golden brown. Let the cookies cool on the baking sheets for 5 minutes. Transfer the cookies to a wire rack and let cool to room temperature before serving.

RYE WALNUT LACE COOKIES

MAKES 16 COOKIES

1 cup rolled rye flakes

¾ cup rye flour

½ teaspoon baking soda

½ teaspoon fine-grain sea salt

½ cup granulated sugar

½ cup light brown sugar

½ cup unsalted butter, melted and cooled

1 large egg

1 teaspoon pure vanilla extract

½ cup finely chopped walnuts

ICING

1½ cups confectioners' sugar, sifted

2 tablespoons milk

Pinch of salt

1 *To make the cookies:* Preheat the oven to 350°F. Line 2 baking sheets with parchment paper.

2 In a medium bowl, mix the rye flakes, rye flour, baking soda, and salt.

3 In a large bowl, whisk the sugars and melted butter until combined. Crack in the egg and pour in the vanilla. Whisk one more time until the egg is thoroughly incorporated. Add the flour mixture in 2 batches, stirring in between additions until combined. Lastly, fold in the walnuts.

4 Using a tablespoon, scoop out balls of dough, spacing them about 2½" from one another on the baking sheets. These cookies spread a lot, so be sure to leave enough room. Bake for 10 to 12 minutes, or until they spread and the edges are lightly golden brown. Allow to cool on the baking sheet for 5 minutes, then carefully move the cookies onto a cooling rack.

5 *To make the icing:* In a medium bowl, whisk together the confectioners' sugar, milk, and salt. When the cookies are cool, drizzle the icing on top in a zigzag motion. Get artsy with it!

BOURBON MILK PUNCH

I'm having a moment with old-school punches. And by old school, I'm talking the ones that were served in speakeasies back when you had to know where the secret door was and recite a password to get in. Contrary to popular opinion, I don't think punches should really pack too much of a "punch." They're supposed to be fun, be easy to drink, and cater to guests who would never in a million years drink liquor straight. Punches are meant to be so delicious that people don't realize they're drinking alcohol. That's when they get in trouble! If you're looking to serve something that will put people on the naughty list, fill a big bowl with this stuff.

MAKES 8 TO 10 SERVINGS

1 cup sugar

1 cup (8 fluid ounces) filtered water

1 stick cinnamon + additional for garnish

¾ cup (6 fluid ounces) whole milk

¾ cup (6 fluid ounces) heavy cream

2 teaspoons pure vanilla extract

1 cup (8 fluid ounces) bourbon

Ground nutmeg

1 In a medium saucepan set over medium heat, combine the sugar, water, and 1 cinnamon stick. Stir until the sugar has dissolved, about 1 minute. Set this simple syrup mixture aside to steep, about 10 minutes. Remove the cinnamon stick and set aside.

2 In a big punch bowl, stir together the whole milk, heavy cream, vanilla, and reserved simple syrup. Lastly, add the bourbon and mix once more.

3 Transfer to the refrigerator to chill. Right before serving, add ice or, if your party is going to last a few hours, serve ice on the side. Add a bit of ground nutmeg and a few cinnamon sticks to garnish.

CINNAMON ROLLS
WITH CREAM CHEESE GLAZE

A lot of recipes don't necessarily mean much to me. I look at them as a list of ratios that yields a product, hopefully a delicious product, but a product nonetheless. But then there are those that are different. You can read a recipe and get a sense of a recipe writer's or chef's way about the kitchen, favorite technique, favorite flavor combinations, what she loves and why. And in a way, through this, you can grasp who they are. This is one of those recipes.

This recipe is adapted from one created by my boyfriend's late mother, pastry chef Amy Pressman. Her cinnamon rolls were voted most popular recipe of 1998 in the Los Angeles Times, *and anyone who knew her always mentions them. Before making these, I had never actually seen a cinnamon roll recipe that called for orange juice and buttermilk. The results are divine! The sweet tartness from those two ingredients makes this dough really special—it works wonders with the cinnamon. Of course, I fiddled with it a little, giving you the option to use brown rice syrup instead of corn syrup and swapping out the topping for a thick and decadent cream cheese glaze. These rolls are just asking to be made on Christmas morning, when presents are being ripped open, coffee is brewing, and the family has gathered.* MAKES 16 ROLLS

(continued)

6 cups all-purpose flour + more for rolling out the dough

½ cup granulated sugar

1 tablespoon fine-grain sea salt

1 cup buttermilk, shaken

1¼ cups orange juice

3 packets (¼ ounce each) dry yeast

2 tablespoons honey

½ cup unsalted butter, cubed, at room temperature

CINNAMON FILLING

3 tablespoons brown rice syrup or light corn syrup

¼ cup ground cinnamon

1½ cups unsalted butter, at room temperature

6 tablespoons granulated sugar

1 tablespoon all-purpose flour

¾ teaspoon salt

1 *To make the rolls:* In the bowl of a stand mixer with the dough hook attachment, mix together the 6 cups of flour, sugar, and salt.

2 Place a small saucepan over medium heat and pour in the buttermilk and orange juice. Heat until lukewarm (100°F), being sure not to overheat or the buttermilk will curdle. Sprinkle the yeast over the buttermilk mixture and stir for 30 seconds, or until it dissolves.

3 Pour the buttermilk mixture into the bowl with the flour and add the honey and softened butter. Mix on low for about 30 seconds, or until all of the ingredients are absorbed into the dough. Keep the mixer going until the dough turns from lumpy to somewhat smooth and elastic, about 5 minutes. Be sure to keep an eye on it the whole time—don't walk away! If the dough appears completely smooth, it's been overworked. Place the dough in a clean, lightly greased bowl. Cover with a clean kitchen towel and let rise in a warm, draft-free area until doubled in bulk, about 1 hour.

4 *To make the cinnamon filling:* In a medium bowl, combine the syrup, cinnamon, butter, sugar, flour, and salt. Using a fork, mash and mix until smooth.

5 *To assemble:* Flour your work surface generously and rolling pin lightly. Divide the dough in half. Roll the first half as evenly as you can into a ½"-thick rectangle. It should be about 10" by 12". Don't be afraid to break out a ruler—cinnamon rolls are important!

CREAM CHEESE GLAZE

8 ounces cream cheese, at room temperature

2 cups confectioners' sugar

½ cup unsalted butter, at room temperature

1 tablespoon pure vanilla extract

Pinch of salt

Splash of milk or water (optional)

6 Using an offset spatula or clean hands, spread half of the cinnamon filling on the surface of the dough rectangle, stopping ½" from the edges. Starting from the opposite long side, roll the dough toward you, snuggly but not so tightly that you push the filling out. When rolled completely, pinch the seam together.

7 With a sharp serrated knife, cut the roll crosswise into buns 1½" thick, using a sawing motion to avoid pressing down on the roll. Transfer the buns to two lightly greased 10" by 10" baking pans and space them about 1" apart. (A variety of baking dishes can be used—use what you have, but be sure to keep them about 1" apart.) They will sort of connect in the oven, but that's totally fine. Repeat this entire process with the remaining dough and filling. Cover the buns with a clean kitchen towel and allow them to rise in a draft-free part of your house until they're puffy and about half again as large. This should take 1 hour.

8 *To make the glaze:* In a medium bowl, using a handheld mixer, mix together the cream cheese, confectioners' sugar, butter, vanilla, and salt. The glaze should be thick yet pourable. If it gets too thick (it might thicken as it sits and waits on the cinnamon rolls), mix in a splash of milk or water.

9 Preheat the oven to 350°F. Uncover the cinnamon rolls and bake for 15 minutes, or until slightly firm to the touch and lightly golden brown. When the cinnamon rolls exit the oven, pour the glaze over them and serve. Rolls will last 3 days when stored in an airtight container, but we all know that ideally they'll be served warm, straight from the oven.

Winter

JANUARY

DO NOTHING

People love to talk about how hard they work. That's all I hear about when I ask for career advice. For the record, I'm okay with hard work. I understand it's a necessity on the road to success, but I wish people would talk more earnestly about the necessity of balancing life and work. When I work endless hours, I need time to do absolutely nothing. I find that hard work requires rest. Doing nothing isn't always easy, but I think that recovery is important; it fuels ideas, inspiration, and peace.

Here are a few things I do when I want to do nothing.

1 I hide my phone. Being constantly connected can lead to anxiety. I can't really explain it, but I'll just say that scrolling through Instagram can sometimes make me feel like I'm not doing enough. In order to completely relax, I place my phone in a dresser drawer and walk away. Unplugging for a few hours always makes me feel like I'm releasing a gigantic exhale.

2 I drink something. Sometimes it ends up being a cocktail and sometimes it's black tea with a splash of milk and a drizzle of honey. I like to sit still in quiet and concentrate on how my drink smells, tastes, and feels. This may sound hokey, but there's something soothing about slowing down physically and mentally and enjoying the simple act of drinking.

3 I watch the clouds, the squirrels, and the trees. When I do nothing, I still like to do *something*, and sometimes that something is to sit in front of my big living room window and watch the squirrels jump from tree to tree.

4 I go on a walk through nature. When I was growing up, my dad always told me he felt closest to God when he was in nature. I never knew what he was talking about until recently. It's hard not to feel connected to the world around you when you're next to trees so tall they seem to touch the sky, birds chirping in their own language, and water cascading down a cliff.

5 I let go of the guilt. I refuse to feel guilty about doing absolutely nothing. By doing nothing, I'm actually giving myself a chance to be more productive and mindful in the future.

Make

FLAVORED BUTTERS

Last year a friend of mine was having an epically bad day. Coincidentally, I had made biscuits with black pepper–strawberry butter for the blog, and after scarfing down a few too many, I was looking for someone to pawn the rest of them off on. It was a perfect fit. I drove to her house and dropped off the care package. Later she told me that butter and biscuits should be given more often in times of need, and I agreed. Of course, it can't be plain butter—that's just boring. It has to be flavored with special and tasty additions. These butters, savory and sweet, can go on so many things: warm breakfast waffles, fluffy biscuits, a piece of crusty bread, a juicy steak, a steaming baked potato . . . really, the options are endless, all proving that butter really does make everything better.

Rosé and Shallot Butter

Chipotle BBQ Bourbon Butter

Nori, Ginger, and Sesame Seed Butter

CHIPOTLE BBQ BOURBON BUTTER (SAVORY)

This recipe was inspired by the famed butter served at the Hog Island Oyster Farm in Point Reyes Station, California, where pats of this glorious business melt atop grilled oysters. It's spicy, a tad sweet, and a teeny bit boozy. This butter would be perfect on a steaming baked potato or smothered on a warm dinner roll. MAKES A HEAPING ¼ CUP

¼ cup bourbon

1 tablespoon light or dark brown sugar

Pinch of fine-grain sea salt

1 clove garlic

2–3 chipotle chile peppers in adobo sauce

¼ cup unsalted butter, at room temperature

1 In a small saucepan, combine the bourbon, sugar, and salt. Bring to a simmer and cook for about 1 minute, or until it reduces by half. Turn off the heat and cool to room temperature.

2 In a food processor, combine the garlic and chipotle peppers and pulse until chopped. Next, add the cooled bourbon mixture and the butter and pulse until completely combined, about 30 seconds.

3 Serve softened or chilled. To chill, transfer the butter to the center of a sheet of plastic wrap. Shape the butter into a log and wrap tightly. Store in the fridge for at least 2 hours.

NORI, GINGER, AND SESAME SEED BUTTER (SAVORY)

This butter has it all: It's briny, like the ocean breeze, and a little spicy thanks to the ginger. Plus, the sesame seeds add a nice nuttiness and texture. I love it on a piece of crusty bread or even a steak for a bit of a surf 'n' turf vibe, but my all-time favorite way to enjoy it is to mix it into a bowl of warm fried rice and drop a runny egg right on top. MAKES ABOUT ¼ CUP

¼ cup unsalted butter, at room temperature

1 tablespoon finely chopped toasted nori (about ¼ sheet)

¾ teaspoon freshly grated ginger

¼ teaspoon sesame seeds

1 To a bowl, add the butter, nori, grated ginger, and sesame seeds. Using a fork, mix until the additions are evenly combined throughout the butter.

2 Serve softened or chilled. To chill, transfer the butter to the center of a sheet of plastic wrap. Shape the butter into a log and wrap tightly. Store in the fridge for at least 2 hours.

ROSÉ AND SHALLOT BUTTER (SAVORY)

This butter is my version of the ubiquitous pinot noir and cabernet butter that seems to grace every menu in Wine Country. Think of this butter as its sprightly and cuter younger sister. This beautifully hued butter tastes light and fresh, just like summer. The shallot gives it a gentle onion flavor, while the rosé provides a slightly sweet and acidic element that would work wonderfully on a steak or even eaten with a bunch of spicy breakfast radishes and a sprinkling of sea salt. MAKES ¼ CUP

½ cup rosé wine, at room temperature

Scant ¼ teaspoon fine-grain sea salt

¼ cup unsalted butter, at room temperature

1 tablespoon finely chopped shallot (about ½ shallot)

1   In a small saucepan over medium-high heat, bring the rosé and salt to a simmer. Cook the rosé until it reduces by three-fourths to 2 tablespoons, about 5 minutes. Pour the reduced rosé into a small bowl and cool to room temperature.

2   Add the butter to a medium bowl. Slowly incorporate the wine into the softened butter, whipping with a fork in between additions. At first it may seem like it won't want to combine, but keep going—it'll eventually get there. Lastly, fold in the shallot.

3   Serve softened or chilled. To chill, transfer the butter to the center of a sheet of plastic wrap. Shape the butter into a log and wrap tightly. Store in the fridge for at least 2 hours.

SALTY HONEY-MATCHA BUTTER (SWEET)

Most teas are dried leaves that are steeped in hot water and then removed. Matcha is different. It's the only tea where the entire leaf is dried and then finely ground so it can be whisked carefully into hot water to make green tea. The results are sublime. It's fragrant, earthy, and rich. Matcha powder isn't cheap, but I find that when I'm baking and cooking with it, the less expensive powder that's labeled "conventional" works great. This butter should be enjoyed for breakfast, on a southern biscuit or on top of a stack of pancakes or a warm, crispy Belgian waffle. **MAKES ¼ CUP**

2 tablespoons honey, divided

½ teaspoon matcha green tea powder

¼ teaspoon fine-grain sea salt

¼ cup unsalted butter, at room temperature

1 In a small bowl, add 1 tablespoon of the honey. Pour in the matcha and whisk vigorously until no lumps are visible. Pour in the remaining 1 tablespoon honey and the salt. Add the butter and mix until completely combined.

2 Serve softened or chilled. To chill, transfer the butter to the center of a sheet of plastic wrap. Shape the butter into a log and wrap tightly. Store in the fridge for at least 2 hours.

STRAWBERRY-ROSE PETAL BUTTER (SWEET)

Floral concoctions like rose water and orange blossom water are usually too overpowering for me. Just one lavender scone can make me feel like Ralphie in A Christmas Story *with a bar of soap in my mouth. Luckily, I discovered dried rose petals, which I find have a delightfully delicate flavor. In this instance, they work wonderfully with sweet strawberries and creamy butter. A dollop of this butter would be a dream on an English scone or slathered on a slice of warm pound cake.* MAKES ¼ CUP

½ cup fresh or frozen and thawed strawberries

2 tablespoons sugar

¼ teaspoon fine-grain sea salt

¼ cup unsalted butter, at room temperature

1 teaspoon crushed rose petals

1 In a saucepan over medium heat, cook the strawberries, sugar, and salt until softened, about 3 to 5 minutes. Pour the strawberry puree through a strainer into a medium bowl. You'll end up with 1 tablespoon.

2 Add the softened butter and beat, using an electric mixer. The butter will appear sloshy and may take a minute to come together, but keep going. Fold in the crushed rose petals.

3 Serve softened or chilled. To chill, transfer the butter to the center of a sheet of plastic wrap. Shape the butter into a log and wrap tightly. Store in the fridge for at least 2 hours.

Tip: Dried edible rose petals can be found in tea shops and gourmet spice stores.

Tip: To dry your own edible rose petals, make sure to use organic roses (no pesticides!). Remove the petals from the stems and spread them out on a baking sheet. The petals will dry from the tips downward. Allow the petals to dry for 2 to 3 days, then store them in an airtight container.

COCONUT RUM BUTTER (SWEET)

If you ever find yourself dreaming about a Caribbean vacation on a dreary day, make this butter and close your eyes. You'll see a sandy beach and yourself wearing heart-shaped sunglasses, holding a piña colada. At least that's what I see. **MAKES ¼ CUP**

3 tablespoons dark rum

1 tablespoon + 1 teaspoon sugar

Pinch of fine-grain sea salt

¼ cup unsalted butter, at room temperature

1 tablespoon shredded unsweetened coconut

1 In a small saucepan set over medium heat, add the rum, sugar, and salt. Cook the rum mixture until it reduces by half, about 2 minutes. Set aside and cool to room temperature.

2 In a medium bowl, place the softened butter. Add the rum mixture in multiple additions, being sure to thoroughly mix between additions. Fold in the coconut.

3 Serve softened or chilled. To chill, transfer the butter to the center of a sheet of plastic wrap. Shape the butter into a log and wrap tightly. Store in the fridge for at least 2 hours.

Coconut Rum Butter

Strawberry-Rose Petal Butter

Do

BIRCH TRIVET

When the temperatures dip, all I want to do is cook stews and braises and drink Hazelnut-Chocolate Hot Toddies (see opposite page). This means I'm using trivets, also known by their less adorable name of "chargers," which are a seasonal necessity. This isn't a fussy DIY by any means. The medium and small birch disks need to be pieced together, almost like a puzzle, but that's it! After that, it's smooth sailing to cozyland.

SUPPLIES

Painter's drop cloth or newspapers

15–20 medium birch disks

12–15 small birch disks

7"-diameter circular wooden plaque

Wood glue

Clear satin fast-drying polyurethane spray

Note: The wooden plaque and birch disks can be found at a craft store, such as Michael's.

1 Lay down a painter's drop cloth or a bed of newspapers to protect your table surface. Arrange the birch disks on the wooden plaque. Move them around so they fit like a puzzle. Place a saucepan on the wooden disks to make sure the positioning is stable. (When I made this trivet, I found that some of the birch disks varied in height. In order to ensure stability when placing a saucepan or pot on the trivet, I positioned the tallest birch disks in the center of the circle.)

2 Lift up the pieces of wood and glue them to the plaque.

3 Place the trivet on your protected table and spray the top with a coat of the clear polyurethane. Allow it to dry completely, about 1 to 2 hours.

HAZELNUT-CHOCOLATE HOT TODDY

When it's cold out . . . let me rephrase that. When it's cold out for Los Angeles, I want nothing more than to curl up to a warm cup of something. The flavors in this hot toddy are very Nutella-like, while the Frangelico (and maybe the bourbon if you're feeling crazy) warms you right up.

MAKES 2 SERVINGS

2 cups very hot water

3 tablespoons unsweetened cocoa powder + additional for garnish

3 tablespoons sugar

½ cup Frangelico liqueur

Whipped cream

Bourbon (optional)

1   In a saucepan set over medium heat, add the hot water, 3 tablespoons cocoa, and sugar. Stir until the sugar dissolves and the mixture is hot.

2   Remove from the heat and stir in the Frangelico. Divide between 2 mugs and top with a dollop of whipped cream and a dusting of cocoa. If you're feeling crazy, add a shot of bourbon to each mug.

VEGETABLE CASSOULET

Traditional cassoulet takes a grand total of 14 to 16 hours (and that doesn't even include soaking the beans overnight). It's a labor of love, requiring time and effort. I'm all about that notion, but sometimes I just want dinner. My cassoulet takes advantage of shortcuts (hello canned beans!). Instead of coaxing the flavors from pork renderings for hours on end, this cassoulet celebrates winter vegetables like squash, leeks, and carrots. MAKES 4 TO 6 SERVINGS

CRUMB TOPPING

1 clove garlic

½ baguette, broken into chunks

2 teaspoons olive oil

Small handful of parsley leaves

¼ teaspoon salt

CASSOULET

3 tablespoons olive oil

2 medium leeks (white and pale green parts only), sliced

3 ribs celery, cut into ½" pieces

3 carrots, cut into 2" pieces

3 cloves garlic, minced

4 sprigs thyme

2 sprigs parsley

2 sprigs tarragon

1 dried bay leaf

1 teaspoon ground cumin

Pinch of ground cloves

1 **To make the crumb topping:** In a food processor, pulse the garlic clove until minced. Add the baguette chunks and pulse until the bread turns into crumbs. Add the oil, parsley leaves, and salt. Pulse once more until the parsley is finely chopped and the topping appears uniform in size.

2 **To make the cassoulet:** In a Dutch oven or large ovenproof pot, heat the oil over medium heat. When the oil is warm and glistens, add the leeks, celery, and carrots. Cook until softened, about 5 minutes.

3 Add the garlic, thyme, parsley, tarragon, bay leaf, cumin, cloves, and tomato paste. Mix and cook until fragrant, about 1 minute.

4 Add the squash and water. Turn up the heat to medium-high and bring the cassoulet to a simmer, then immediately turn the heat to medium-low and cover the pot. Cook for 15 to 20 minutes, or until the carrots and squash are tender.

(continued)

3 tablespoons tomato paste

1 cup cubed peeled
butternut squash
(½ butternut squash)

2 cups water

Salt

2 cans (15 ounces each)
great Northern beans

5　Preheat the oven to 350°F. Give the cassoulet a taste test and add salt to your liking. Mix in the beans and, using a wooden spoon, smooth the top of the cassoulet and sprinkle the crumb topping over it.

6　Transfer the pot, uncovered, to the oven to bake for 10 to 15 minutes, or until the top is crispy and golden brown. Ladle into bowls and eat warm with additional bread, if you like.

Live

WRITE HANDWRITTEN NOTES

It isn't every year that I can send out holiday cards. Sometimes the season is so chaotic that before I know it, I'm welcoming the new year. If this happens, I like to set some time aside in January, when the craziness of the holiday is behind me and moments of quiet are easier to find, to write thoughtful notes to the people who mean the most.

In a day when communication is mostly through e-mail, texts, tweets, and Facebook messages, I know my friends are stoked to open their mailboxes, amid the bills and catalogs and junk mail, to see a note from me, thanking them for being in my life.

Do

ORGANIZE YOUR PANTRY

Have you ever gone to organize your pantry and realized you need, like, a million dollars to buy all of those fancy plastic containers? Me, too—though I like to stick to glass jars that I can buy in bulk. It's an investment, it really is, but having things in order makes my crazy brain a little less loony. I find that when I'm moving swiftly through the kitchen, organization is key. It's less frustrating and makes for a much more enjoyable cooking experience.

SUPPLIES

Assorted jars (Mason jars are economical)

Labels (I like washi tape or brown tape)

Baskets

Cake stands

Trivets

Wooden shelves

1 Find your vessels. I find that Mason jars are the most economical. I also like saving used pickle and jam jars. And I just adore the shape of Weck jars.

2 Make a list of everything that needs a home and how much of it you have. Let's talk labels: I used brown tape I found online, but washi tape or even plain masking tape will work. And since I'm a bit OCD, I like to cut my tape in even strips so everything looks uniform. Gather your jars and label them accordingly. (You know how to do this!) Fill the corresponding jar, seal it, and you're done!

3 Create zones. I like to group together grains, flours, spices, and so on, which makes it easy when I'm in search of something.

4 Use baskets, cake stands, and trivets. I'll stash odds and ends that don't fit in jars on cake stands or hide them away in apple orchard baskets.

ROTISSERIE CHICKEN THREE WAYS

When I was growing up, my parents very rarely ordered takeout, although a store-bought rotisserie chicken with quickly thrown together sides was always in heavy rotation.

A rotisserie chicken can make dinner a breeze, which is great because it's a rare occasion in which I actually want to roast a chicken myself (a big exception is the Beer Can Pollo a la Brasa on page 213). So, just like my mom, I opt for the store-bought variety. This collection of recipes gives you three very different dinner options, all simply using one (3-pound) store-bought rotisserie chicken. Shred the chicken, save the carcass (we use that to make the broth for chicken and dumplings—no waste!), and you're on your way. The flavors from each recipe are very different, but they're all comforting and fall into the perfect, no-fuss category that everyone is craving during the start of the year.

CHICKEN GYROS
WITH TZATZIKI SAUCE

MAKES 2 SERVINGS

½ red onion, thinly sliced

1 cup white distilled or red wine vinegar

1 teaspoon sugar

1 teaspoon + a few pinches of salt

¼ cup plain Greek yogurt

2 tablespoons sour cream

1 tablespoon finely chopped fresh dill

1 tablespoon finely chopped fresh Italian parsley + additional for serving

1 Persian cucumber, cut into small cubes

Juice from 1 lemon

1 cup shredded cooked chicken

4 pitas

Lettuce (optional)

1   To quickly pickle the red onion, pour the vinegar, sugar, and 1 teaspoon salt into a small saucepan. Bring to a simmer over medium-high heat. Add the red onion to a jar and pour the pickling liquid over it. Allow to stand for at least 30 minutes. Store, covered, in the fridge for 6 months to a year.

2   Meanwhile, preheat the oven to 250°F. In a small bowl, whisk together the yogurt, sour cream, dill, 1 tablespoon parsley, cucumber, lemon juice, and a few pinches of salt.

3   Warm up the chicken and pitas by placing them in the oven on a sheet of foil. I like to serve this as a "make-your-own" dish. On a large platter, arrange the warmed shredded chicken, pitas, tzatziki sauce, pickled red onion, and some additional Italian parsley or lettuce, if desired.

Chicken and
Dumplings

Chicken Gyros
with Tzatziki Sauce

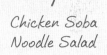

Chicken Soba
Noodle Salad

CHICKEN SOBA NOODLE SALAD

4 ounces dried soba noodles

2 tablespoons rice wine vinegar

2 tablespoons low-sodium soy sauce (see note)

1 teaspoon sesame oil

½ teaspoon sugar

1 clove garlic, minced

¾ teaspoon grated fresh ginger

1 cup shredded chicken breast

3 scallions, thinly sliced

Small handful of cilantro leaves

½ teaspoon sesame seeds

Note: Low-sodium soy sauce is a must in this recipe. If you only have regular soy sauce, then decrease the amount to 1 tablespoon or the salad will be a bit too salty.

1 Cook the soba noodles in salted boiling water until they're tender yet still firm, about 3 to 5 minutes. Drain the noodles and immediately run them under cold water to stop any additional cooking. Give them a good shake in the colander and set them aside.

2 In a small bowl, whisk together the rice wine vinegar, soy sauce, sesame oil, sugar, garlic, and ginger.

3 Place the noodles in a medium bowl and pour the vinegar dressing over them. If the noodles have chilled, they may have started to stick together—not to worry: Take a fork and mix in the dressing vigorously. This will help separate the noodles.

4 Toss in the shredded chicken. Garnish with the scallions, cilantro, and sesame seeds. If you have any leftovers, the noodles will keep well in the fridge. Just before serving, add a few teaspoons of sesame oil since the noodles tend to soak up a lot of the dressing.

Tip: Most packages of dried soba noodles recommend a cooking time of 6 to 8 minutes. I find that if you want tender yet firm noodles, 6 to 8 minutes is way too long. I usually boil mine for about 3 minutes. Since every set of noodles is slightly different, I say give them a taste at the 3-minute mark and decide whether they're cooked to your liking.

CHICKEN AND DUMPLINGS

1 tablespoon olive oil

½ shallot, finely chopped

1 rib celery, thinly sliced

1 small carrot, finely chopped

1 sprig thyme

1 quart filtered water

1 rotisserie chicken carcass

¾ cup all-purpose flour

1 teaspoon baking powder

½ teaspoon fine-grain sea salt + more to taste

½ cup buttermilk, shaken

1½ cups shredded chicken

Freshly ground black pepper

1 In a medium pot set over medium heat, heat the oil. When the oil glistens, add the shallot, celery, and carrot. Mix in the thyme sprig. Cook until the vegetables are softened, about 3 minutes.

2 Pour in the water and place the chicken carcass in the center. Bring the water to a simmer and cover the pot. Cook for 15 to 20 minutes, or until very fragrant.

3 Meanwhile, make the dumplings. In a small bowl, whisk together the flour, baking powder, and ½ teaspoon of salt. Pour in the buttermilk and mix until just combined.

4 Remove the carcass from the water and discard. At this time the broth should be flavorful and fragrant. Give it a taste and adjust the seasoning according to your liking. I added about ½ teaspoon of salt. Depending on the rotisserie chicken you're using, you may need to skim the top of the broth to remove some of the fat. Personally, I like some fat—it adds great flavor!

5 Bring the broth to a medium boil. Drop a heaping tablespoon of dough right onto the bubbling point. (The extreme heat from that bubbling point reacts with the baking powder in the dough to create a really fluffy dumpling.) Continue until you've worked your way through all of the dough. You should end up with about 5 dumplings. Cover the pot so the dumplings can cook for about 2 to 3 minutes.

6 Carefully move the dumplings aside and slide the shredded chicken into the broth. Divide the dumplings and broth between 2 bowls and serve with a sprinkling of black pepper.

START A GOOD HABIT

Starting a bad habit is much easier than starting a good one. In the third grade I had a nasty routine of chewing my nails; my mother quickly snapped me out of that one. She used one part "mom lecture" and another part pure bribery (I had a strong love affair with the toys that came with Happy Meals). Beginning a good habit takes planning, commitment, and realistic expectations. In the last year, I started working out regularly, and to my surprise, I actually stuck with it! Here's what worked for me.

1 Setting small goals. When I committed to working out, I knew the only way I'd be successful was if I made it realistic and attainable. At the time, my workload was heavy and I knew that three times a week, maximum, would have to do. To my surprise, I ended up wanting to work out more!

2 Being consistent. Sometimes mere completion is better than perfection. I found this to be very true when starting to exercise. The workouts I did weren't always flawless, but I completed them. And then I tried hard not to ruin my hard work with doughnuts. The struggle is real.

3 Creating rewards. From simple rewards like an almond cappuccino to a hair appointment at Drybar, all gave me incentive to throw on my workout clothes and just get it done.

4 Having low expectations. It helped a lot that I didn't go into it wishing and hoping I'd end up with a six-pack. Instead, my intention was to feel healthy, burn off a bit of stress, and fit into my favorite pair of jeans that didn't fit me anymore because of one reason and only one reason: writing a book about pancakes.

FEBRUARY

Live

VISIT A TEA SHOP

Is there anything more cozy than warming up to a cup of hot tea on a cold day? The answer is no way. For years I was strictly a black tea drinker (I love PG Tips!), but I've recently broadened my horizons and been on a quest to try a variety of teas. The first step in trying new-to-me teas was a trip to a tea shop. Tea shopping is like anything that's very niche: It can sort of be intimidating, especially when you don't know how to start. Here's what I learned on my trip to the tea shop.

1　Most tea is priced by weight, but luckily for us, it's pretty affordable. I balked at the price of $40 a pound, but I quickly realized that I only needed an ounce (a pound is a *ton* of tea!).

2　Tell the shopkeeper how you like your coffee and what your favorite foods and flavors are. Do you like strong and robust coffee? You may like black teas from China or India. Do you like flavors that are more delicate and nuanced?

You may find that different types of rooibos and white teas are more your style. Do you like floral notes and berries? Teas like chrysanthemum, jasmine, and lily might be to your liking.

3　Tell the shopkeeper how you want tea to make you feel. Alive and invigorated? Calm and subdued? Sleepy? There are endless varieties and blends that will cater to any of these wants.

CRAB GRAPEFRUIT GRANITA SALAD

A few years ago I dipped into one of my favorite New York restaurants, Northern Spy, for a quiet dinner with one of my best friends. We ordered the ubiquitous kale and beet salad that seemed to be on every winter menu that year. As we dug in, we quickly realized that this salad looked like every other kale salad but was way different. Underneath a leaf of kale was a pretty quenelle of beet sorbet! Up until that point, I'd never eaten sorbet in a savory context before. I absolutely loved the idea. So I riffed on that notion here, instead opting to include a version of the shaved ice Italian dessert, the granita. This granita, unlike most, doesn't have any sugar—we're going for savory this time—but it does require the process of scraping the grapefruit ice to get a fluffy, icy texture. The pockets of cold, flavored ice are such a delightful surprise next to the creamy avocado, briny crab, and segments of tart and sweet pomelo. MAKES 4 SERVINGS

1½ cups ruby red grapefruit juice (from 2 large grapefruits)

Salt

3 king crab legs

Juice from ½ lemon

1 tablespoon olive oil

Ground black pepper

1 bulb fennel with fronds still attached

1 pomelo, segmented

1 avocado, finely chopped

1 Pour the grapefruit juice into a small bowl and mix in a pinch of salt. Freeze for 2 hours. When the juice is frozen, scrape with a fork until a fluffy granita forms. Transfer back to the freezer until you're ready to serve.

2 Bring a pot of salted water to a boil over high heat. Add the crab legs and boil for 3 to 4 minutes. Open the legs using a pair of kitchen shears, remove the crabmeat, and chop it into bite-size pieces.

3 In a medium bowl, mix together the lemon juice, oil, and a pinch each of salt and pepper.

4 Let's prep the fennel! Cut the fennel bulb in half and remove the green center. Using a mandoline (or very sharp knife), thinly slice half of the fennel bulb. Repeat the slicing with the second half. Pluck off a few fronds and set them aside—we're going to use them for a garnish.

5 To the bowl of dressing, add the sliced fennel, pomelo, and reserved pieces of crabmeat and toss. Divide among 4 plates. Top with the avocado and garnish with the fennel fronds. Lastly, spoon a heaping mound of granita onto each plate.

Note: During this season, winter citrus will be everywhere, including most farmers' markets and grocery stores. The flavor of a pomelo can be compared to that of a grapefruit, though it is less bitter and a teeny bit sweeter.

Make

BLOOD ORANGE GIN-GIN MULES

*I love a good Moscow mule, but since I'm more of a gin drinker, I prefer to make them with gin.
Blood orange juice gives this drink a beautiful hue and a sweetness I adore.* MAKES 4

½ cup sugar

½ cup (4 fluid ounces) water

1" knob peeled fresh ginger, sliced into coins

Ice cubes

1 cup (8 fluid ounces) blood orange juice (from about 8 blood oranges)

¾ cup (6 fluid ounces) gin

Tonic water

1 In a medium saucepan set over medium-low heat, warm the sugar and water until the sugar dissolves. Add the ginger. Bring to a simmer and then immediately turn off the heat. Allow to steep for 10 minutes.

2 *To assemble the drinks:* Add a few ice cubes to each of 4 glasses and pour in 2 tablespoons (1 ounce) of the ginger syrup. Divide the blood orange juice among the glasses and top each with 3 tablespoons (1½ ounces) of gin and a liberal splash of tonic water. Give 'em a stir and serve.

Do

DOORMAT WITH A MESSAGE

I've come to the conclusion that all of the cutest doormats in the world are expensive. Sorry, pricey doormats, you're at the very bottom of my splurge list. Luckily for us, I've found that cute-ifying a plain one couldn't be simpler. It starts with a dreaded trip to IKEA (please get a soft-serve at the end—it makes it all better). And then, from there, it's just paint and a bit of patience.

SUPPLIES

Pen or pencil

Thick stock paper

X-ACTO knife

Plain jute doormat

Colored acrylic spray paint

Clear varnish top coat spray

1 Using a pen or pencil, draw your stenciled message in block letters on the stock paper. Using the knife, carefully cut out the stencil. (Or, if you like, feel free to use a store-bought stencil.)

2 Place the stencil atop the doormat and position it where you like.

3 Secure the stencil with one hand and, with the other, spray-paint the negative space of the stencil. Allow to dry completely, about 1 hour.

4 Remove the stencil and spray the doormat with a top coat. Allow the doormat to dry for an additional 30 minutes to 1 hour before stepping on it.

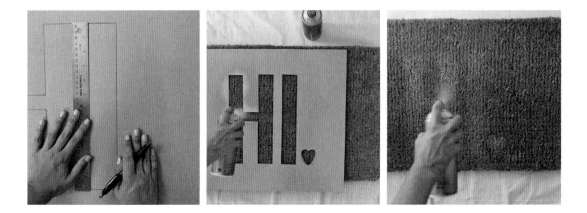

Pretty citrus
cures winter blues.

ORANGE–THYME UPSIDE-DOWN CAKE

Hello, you showstopper, you! The intention of this cake is to brighten up a dreary, cold winter day. The best accompaniments to this cake are a cup of warm tea and an all-consuming book; think something by Gillian Flynn or Tana French. **MAKES ONE 12" CAKE**

CAKE

2 cups all-purpose flour

1¾ teaspoons baking powder

½ teaspoon fine-grain sea salt

½ cup unsalted butter, at room temperature

½ cup granulated sugar

2 large eggs

1 teaspoon pure vanilla extract

¾ cup whole milk

WINTER CITRUS TOPPING

¼ cup unsalted butter

3 sprigs thyme, stems removed and discarded

½ cup light brown sugar

¼ teaspoon fine-grain sea salt

4 blood oranges, peeled and cut into slices

2 Cara Cara or navel oranges, peeled and cut into slices

Whipped cream

1 *To make the cake:* Preheat the oven to 350°F. In a medium bowl, mix together the flour, baking powder, and salt.

2 Next, in the bowl of a standing mixer with the paddle attachment, cream together the butter and sugar until light and fluffy, about 1 minute. Add the eggs and vanilla, and beat until thoroughly incorporated.

3 Stir half the flour mixture and all of the milk into the butter and sugar mixture. Then stir in the remaining flour mixture, being sure not to overmix. At this point, the batter will probably look like it's curdled. Not to worry. This is not a smooth batter, but it will come together splendidly in the oven.

4 *To make the topping:* In a seasoned 10" cast-iron skillet, melt the butter over medium heat. Mix in the thyme, brown sugar, and salt and stir until the sugar begins to bubble, about 1 minute. Turn off the heat and let stand for a few minutes to cool slightly.

5 Arrange the orange slices, overlapping a few of them, on top of the brown sugar mixture. Pour the cake batter over the citrus slices, and spread the batter gently so it's nice and even. Transfer the skillet to the oven and bake for 35 to 45 minutes, or until a wooden pick comes out clean.

6 Remove the cake from the oven and allow to cool on a wire rack for 5 to 10 minutes. To invert the cake, run a knife along the outside edge of the cake, place a plate on top of the cast-iron skillet, and turn both of them over—be careful, they'll be heavy! Lift up the skillet and voilà! Your cake! Serve this cake slightly warm with a dollop of soft whipped cream.

Do

SHIBORI TIE-DYED TABLE RUNNER

I fell in love with tie-dyeing at summer camp. I was a tragic tie-dyer, though, mixing colors of green, yellow, blue, and pink—basically, the more colors the better! I think differently now that I'm grown up. I like to go with one or two colors at most. The Japanese tie-dye technique called shibori takes it to a whole new and beautiful level. This particular type of shibori utilizes two square pieces of wood, which are tightly fastened onto either end of the fabric in order to create smaller squares of negative space, while the folds in the fabric remain dyed. I mixed two colors together—a petal pink and fuchsia—but get creative with it and use whatever color or colors you like. I think a warm gray, lilac, or mint green would also be really beautiful.

SUPPLIES

Pair of rubber gloves

5-quart plastic bucket

3½ quarts warm water

1 tablespoon salt

Powdered dye (I used 1 part fuchsia and 1 part petal pink from Rit)

White linen (mine measured 17½" x 52")

2 wooden squares (mine measured 8" x ¼")

4 rubber bands

Scissors

Iron

Fabric glue or fabric tape (optional)

1 Put on your rubber gloves and fill your plastic bucket with the warm water. Pour in the salt and then the dye and stir until combined. (I added about one-quarter packet of fuchsia powdered dye and one-quarter packet of petal pink.) Remove your gloves and set them aside.

2 Next, fold the linen like you would a business letter: into thirds, lengthwise. Fold in the other direction like an accordion: under, over, under, over. Repeat until the linen looks like a stack of squares. Place the 2 wooden squares on opposite sides of the linen square and secure them with the rubber bands. Make sure the rubber bands are tight, as this will ensure that little to no dye gets into the center of the fabric.

(continued)

3 Put on your gloves and dip the linen into the dye. Allow it to sit for about a minute.

4 Remove the linen from the dye and, without removing the rubber bands, allow it to dry completely, ideally overnight. Lastly, rinse the linen under cold water until the water runs clear. Remove the rubber bands using a pair of scissors. Hang to dry.

5 Lightly iron the linen on a very low setting. I don't like to iron it too much because I love linen's wrinkly attributes. This last step is entirely optional, but if you don't like the frayed edges (I personally love them), fold over the edges and iron the seam. Apply the fabric glue or tape along the underside of the seam and press firmly until married.

TAKE PHOTOS OF YOUR FOOD

What is it about documenting what we eat that is so fascinating? It just is. A good food photo has the ability to transport others to your table, leaving them drooling and wishing they were eating whatever you've just artfully displayed. Here are some tips I've learned for achieving a drool-worthy food photo.

1 Shoot with natural, indirect light. Unless you're Terry Richardson, trying to make food look sexy, never turn on your flash. Instead, shoot by a window using indirect sunlight. Pay attention to the direction of the light, too. Are you shooting a drink? Shoot into the light! Light streaming through drinks looks oh so pretty.

2 Don't shoot food too closely. Back up. If you're too close, people can't see the actual food. I want to see the world in which you eat. I want to see the plate, the drink you're having with the food, the fork you are using. I want the whole world, not just a sliver of it.

3 If you're shooting on your phone, which most likely has a wide-angle lens, you might notice that shooting straight on creates a bit of a fish-eye effect—you see too much and things are a bit warped. If this is happening, opt to position the camera at a three-quarters angle (slightly higher than straight on) or directly overhead.

4 Use props. Don't feel shy about moving plates and glasses around or putting a fork in the right place.

5 Use filters with restraint. This isn't the 1970s! Various apps out there, including Instagram, allow you to apply a filter, and then bring it down a notch. Do this!

GRAVLAX

I will forever and ever be a carb-lover. I love pasta and gnocchi and bread and pancakes and, of course, bagels. Oh, bagels. I'm not sure I've ever met a bagel I didn't love. Correction: I've never met a New York bagel I didn't love. I love my New York bagels smothered in soft cream cheese, topped with slices of salmon, red onion, and a few capers. Recently, instead of the usual smoked salmon, I've been all about cured salmon, also known as gravlax. This version has bits of fennel, pink peppercorns, fresh dill, and lemon. It also has a teeny hint of gin, which adds the subtle flavor of juniper berries that I find to be crazy delicious. MAKES 6 TO 8 SERVINGS

4–6 pink peppercorns

½ teaspoon fennel seeds

1 tablespoon salt

2 tablespoons sugar

Zest of 1 lemon

Handful of finely chopped fresh dill

1 tablespoon gin

1 pound sushi-grade salmon, pin bones removed

Tip: Be sure to ask the fishmonger to remove the pin bones for you. If you forget, you can simply pull them out using a pair of kitchen tweezers.

1 In a small skillet set over medium heat, toast the peppercorns and fennel seeds for 1 to 2 minutes, or until fragrant, giving the skillet a good shake from time to time. Transfer to a mortar and pestle and add the salt, sugar, and lemon peel. Crush and twist and crush and twist again until the mixture is ground up. Alternatively, if you don't have a mortar and pestle, you could crush the spices on a cutting board with the back of a chef's knife.

2 Mix the dill and gin into the salt and spice mixture. Spread the mixture, in 1 layer, on the exposed surface of the salmon. Wrap the salmon very tightly in a few sheets of plastic wrap and transfer, skin side down, to a baking dish. Place in the refrigerator to cure for 24 hours.

(continued)

Bagels

Cream cheese

Thinly sliced watermelon radishes

Capers

Sliced cucumbers

Dill fronds

Lemon wedges

Sliced red onion

Rye toasts

Mustard

3 Unwrap the fish and remove the salmon from the liquid and spices it will now be surrounded by. Rub off and discard the dill and extra spices to expose the pink salmon flesh. Transfer the salmon to a cutting board. Using a serrated or very sharp knife, thinly slice, on the diagonal, slithers of the salmon. Perfection is not necessary here—just try your best to slice it as thinly as possible.

4 Serve the gravlax on bagels with sides of cream cheese, thinly sliced watermelon radishes, capers, and sliced cucumbers, if desired. Or you can go the more traditional route and serve it with rye toasts and a bit of mustard, or use the toppings of your choice.

A VALENTINE'S DAY MESS

Valentine's Day isn't everyone's favorite holiday. If you're single, it can feel more like Singles Awareness Day. And if you're in a relationship, the cheap candy, wine, or champagne can also be kind of saccharine. My vote, regardless of relationship status, is to stay home, put on some pj's, watch some trashy television, and eat dessert. This recipe is a play on the British dessert known as Eton mess. There are chunks of warm-brownie goodness, crispy shattered bits of meringue, perfectly whipped cream, a dusting of pistachios, and—since I'm a lover of hot and cold—a few scoops of ice cream. This dessert is enough for two, but it can also be enjoyed solo depending on, well, how messy your Valentine's Day is. MAKES 1 OR 2 SERVINGS

MERINGUE

1 large egg white

1 teaspoon vinegar

Pinch of salt

¼ teaspoon cornstarch or ½ teaspoon tapioca starch

2 tablespoons sugar

Tip: Good meringues show up at the bakeries this time of year; feel free to skip a step and use store-bought meringues, if you're looking to save a bit of time.

1   *To make the meringue:* Preheat the oven to 200°F. Line a baking sheet with parchment paper.

2   In a stainless steel bowl, using an electric mixer, beat the egg white, vinegar, and pinch of salt until the white turns frothy. With the mixer going, add the cornstarch or tapioca starch and then pour in the sugar, a little at a time, until the mixture looks shiny, like a pretty girl's hair. Keep beating the egg white until it doubles in volume and stiff peaks form, about 3 to 5 minutes.

3   Scoop out the meringue and place it in the center of the parchment paper. Smooth it out so it's an even layer that's about 1" high. Place the meringue in the oven, keeping the door to the oven open just a few inches. Bake for 3 to 4 hours, or until the meringue is dry and crisp on the top. Allow the meringue to cool completely on a wire rack.

4   Peel the meringue off the parchment paper and break it into pieces. (The meringue can be made up to 3 days before and kept in an airtight container.)

(continued)

2 tablespoons unsalted butter

2 ounces dark chocolate, chopped

¼ cup sugar

½ teaspoon pure vanilla extract

¼ cup all-purpose flour

¼ teaspoon salt

2 tablespoons whole milk

1 large egg yolk

Whipped cream

Handful of chopped pistachios

Ice cream of choice (I used coffee ice cream)

5 *To make the brownie:* Preheat the oven to 350°F. Grease, flour, and line an 8½" x 4½" loaf pan with parchment paper.

6 Create a makeshift double boiler by placing a glass or stainless steel bowl atop a saucepan filled with a few inches of water, being sure the water isn't touching the bottom of the bowl. Add the butter and chocolate to the bowl and turn the heat to high. When the chocolate has melted, stir until very smooth.

7 In a medium bowl, mix together the melted chocolate mixture, sugar, and vanilla. Next, add the flour and salt. Give it a good mix and then pour in the milk and add the egg yolk. Mix one last time and then transfer the brownie batter to the prepared loaf pan.

8 Bake for 12 to 15 minutes, or until the edges have set and the top appears a bit crackly. Allow the brownie to cool slightly, just until you can handle it, about 3 to 4 minutes. Slice it up into cubes. The center will still be a bit gooey.

9 *To assemble the mess:* Place a generous smear of whipped cream on the plate. Arrange the cubes of brownie bites all over— get artsy with it. Top with the shattered pieces of meringue, chopped pistachios, and scoops of ice cream. There's no wrong way to do this!

Live

START A COLLECTION

When I think of a great collector, Ariel from *The Little Mermaid* immediately pops into my head. *"Look at this stuff, isn't it neat?"* She was a collector, yes, but she was also a bit of a hoarder, wasn't she? I'm convinced there's a way to collect something and not have it consume your whole house. I've recently started a new collection, and these are a few tips I found to be helpful.

1 Collect something that you'll actually use or that you find interesting. Vintage ice cream scoops came naturally to me. I was in search of one, and since I came across so many that I loved, I figured why not collect them all? It also helps that ice cream is one of my favorite things ever.

2 Collect casually. This is easy for me because I oftentimes pop into vintage or thrift stores to take a look around, but I believe collecting something shouldn't be too much work. It should be a slow and enjoyable process.

3 Buy quality stuff. I don't buy ice cream scoops that have broken handles or chips or crazy nicks. I try to buy interesting, beautiful ice cream scoops. That way, I'll actually want to display them in my house. And, even more important, I can use them!

MARCH

IDEAS FOR ENJOYING EARLY MORNINGS

I'm not much of a morning person. I don't naturally spring out of bed at the first sliver of sunlight. I need an alarm—and I need a loud one. Oddly enough, my mornings have become the most sacred part of my day. I like to get up a few hours before the e-mails start pouring in, before Amelia's barking and whining commence, and before the whole world is bustling. This quiet time, while short-lived and scarce, sets me up for a good day. Here are some tips that have helped me enjoy my mornings.

1 Drink coffee. Drink a smoothie. Or even lemon water. Basically, create a routine around some consumption. I go to bed dreaming about my morning cup of coffee and oatmeal.

2 Prepare the night before. I write my daily to-do list the night before. This means I don't have to wrack my brain figuring out what I have to get done. Instead, I can run on autopilot until I wake up—aka until my coffee kicks in.

3 Banish technology. It takes a tremendous amount of self-discipline to not immediately check my phone the minute my eyes open. Since I have no self-discipline whatsoever, I've resorted to keeping my phone in the other room.

4 Go on a walk. The best part about having a dog is my early morning walks. Everything from feeling the chilly air to seeing the sun rise through the trees provides a sense of peace before the start of the day.

BENTO BOXES

For years my favorite place to dip into for a quick and easy lunch was a very nondescript Japanese restaurant near my work. I'd always order the bento box, which would come in a traditional bento box tray with compartments for small portions of delicious and healthy foods: seaweed salads, grilled salmon, rice, spicy cucumber salad. The lineup would change daily; the ever-rotating menu made me excited for lunch and didn't leave me bored the way a deli sandwich often does. These ideas for bento boxes are all easy to make, are mostly healthy and light (who wants to be bogged down by lunch?), and will keep well in your office fridge. Even now, as a person who works from home, I love preparing one the night before or the morning of and having it ready for a relaxing lunch break.

1ST BENTO BOX

I'm having a moment with sprouts: pumpkin sprouts, broccoli sprouts, radish sprouts— I even love good ol' throwback alfalfa sprouts. They make any sandwich better, especially with smashed avocado. And don't even get me started on how much I love ants on a log.

AVOCADO SANDWICH WITH SPROUTS

In a bowl, smash an avocado with the juice from half a lemon and a few pinches of salt. Spoon onto a slice of lightly toasted multigrain bread and top the avocado with a heavy hand of sprouts. Place the second slice of bread on top.

SNOW PEAS

In a small bowl, whisk together a teaspoon of sesame oil and a teaspoon of rice wine vinegar. Add about ½ cup of snow peas and toss until coated. Add a few pinches of sesame seeds and toss once more.

GROWN-UP ANTS ON A LOG

Slice up a few ribs of celery. Fill with a teaspoon or two of almond butter, cashew butter, or my absolute favorite—all-natural crunchy peanut butter. Top with a few golden raisins.

Try this sandwich
open-faced, too!

A tuna niçoise salad, bento-box style.

Breakfast meets lunch

2ND BENTO BOX

This is like a torn-apart tuna niçoise salad on a piece of grilled bread. It's fresh and light yet still has the ability to cure my hangries.

SEARED AHI TUNA ON GRILLED BREAD

Rub a teaspoon of olive oil on the soft inside of a baguette piece. Place it on the burner grate of a gas stove and turn the flame to medium. Toast on all sides. In a small skillet over medium-high heat, heat a few tablespoons of olive oil. When the oil is hot, add 2 ounces of sushi-grade tuna, searing on all sides for about 30 seconds. Remove and slice with a very sharp knife. Arrange on the grilled bread. In a teeny bowl, make the gremolata. Add a few tablespoons of finely chopped Italian parsley, a few capers, and a few pinches of salt. Top the tuna with the gremolata.

BOILED EGG

In a small saucepan, cover an egg with water. Place over high heat. Once the water begins to boil, turn off the heat and cover the pan. Let stand for 8 to 9 minutes. Run under cold water and peel. Slice and arrange in the bento box.

OTHER FUN ADDITIONS

Chop up some cherry tomatoes, add some olives, and boil up a few baby potatoes.

3RD BENTO BOX

This bento box is a celebration of my favorite protein: eggs. No matter the day, I can always depend on having a few on hand. I love to rewarm this frittata and potato salad in a toaster oven for a few minutes.

HERBED BABY FRITTATA

In a small bowl, whisk together 2 large eggs, ¼ teaspoon of salt, and a few teaspoons of finely chopped fresh basil, chives, and flat-leaf Italian parsley. Preheat the oven to 300°F. Pour the egg mixture into a small ramekin. Make sure it can fit into your bento box. Transfer the ramekin to the center of a baking sheet and bake for 20 to 25 minutes, or until the edges of the frittata are lightly golden brown and the center has risen slightly.

GERMAN BABY POTATO SALAD

Halve a handful of fingerling potatoes. Boil them in salted water until tender, about 5 to 7 minutes. Drain. In a small bowl, whisk together 2 teaspoons of red wine vinegar, 1 teaspoon of olive oil, and a teaspoon of whole grain mustard. Add the potatoes and salt and pepper to taste.

CUCUMBERS AND TOMATOES

Slice up half of a Persian cucumber and halve a handful of cherry tomatoes. Toss with the juice from half a lemon and a few pinches of salt and pepper.

Do

HAND-PAINTED PILLOW

One of the easiest ways to gussy up a chair is by adding a pillow. It can add a nice pop of personality, color, and pattern; I like to think of them as living room flare. Since I'm a bit averse to sewing, I like to simply buy plain white pillow covers and paint them in cute colors and patterns. I'm no Picasso, so I like to keep it simple with shapes I know I can paint, like polka dots, raindrop shapes, plus marks, and waves.

SUPPLIES

Paintbrush

Fabric paint

20" x 20" plain white pillow cover

Clear acrylic coating spray

22" x 22" pillow insert (see note)

Note: I recommend buying a pillow insert that's a few inches bigger than the pillow cover. This will make the pillow appear full and fluffy.

1 Decide on the pattern you'd like to make: polka dots, raindrop shapes, plus marks, waves, chevrons—get creative! If your pillow cover is wrinkled, feel free to give it a good ironing. And then use your paintbrush and fabric paint to paint the pillow cover.

2 Allow to dry completely, about 2 to 3 hours, and then spray with the top coat. Dry for an additional hour.

3 At this time, your pillow cover will be dry enough for people to lean against it. Fill the cover with the pillow insert and decorate your favorite chair with it.

I found my plain white pillow cover at IKEA.

You can use a 9" x 5"
loaf pan; the bread will
just be a bit stouter.

SEEDED, NUTTY BANANA BREAD

Some may argue that the coziest of cozy foods is warm banana bread. I'd say they're right! I have a bit of a bratitude when it comes to banana bread. For starters, I don't like it too moist (we all hate that word, don't we?), and I like it to be studded with loads of seeds and walnuts. Oh, and dark rum, too! The glory of banana bread is that it can be eaten slowly, a few slices a day, and then wrapped up and revisited the next day, and the day after that. Of course, that's if you can resist eating it all in one sitting. **MAKES ONE 8½" X 4½" LOAF**

BREAD

1½ cups all-purpose flour

2 tablespoons sunflower seeds

3 tablespoons millet seeds

¾ cup chopped walnuts

¾ teaspoon salt

⅓ cup melted unsalted butter

¼ cup light brown sugar

¼ cup granulated sugar

1 large egg

1 teaspoon pure vanilla extract

2 tablespoons dark rum

3 ripe yet firm bananas, mashed

1 teaspoon baking soda

TOPPING

1 banana, sliced horizontally (see photo)

1 teaspoon sunflower seeds

1 teaspoon millet seeds

1 *To make the bread:* Preheat the oven to 350°F. Butter and flour an 8½" x 4½" loaf pan.

2 In a medium bowl, mix the flour, sunflower seeds, millet seeds, walnuts, and salt until combined.

3 In a large bowl, whisk together the melted butter and sugars. Crack in the egg, pour in the vanilla and rum, and mix until thoroughly combined. Add the mashed bananas and baking soda and give it another good stir.

4 Add the flour mixture to the butter mixture, stirring just until the speckles of flour disappear. Be sure to scrape the bottom of the bowl to get any bits of flour that might be hiding. Pour the batter into the prepared loaf pan. Give the pan a couple of moderate smacks on the counter to even out the batter.

5 *To make the topping:* Arrange the banana slices on top of the bread and sprinkle the sunflower seeds and millet seeds around the bananas.

6 Bake for 45 to 50 minutes, or until the center has risen, the edges are golden brown, and a skewer inserted into the center comes out clean. Allow the bread to cool for 5 minutes in the pan, then invert the loaf and cool it on a rack, or live on the edge and eat it warm. The banana bread will stay delicious and moist for 3 to 5 days when wrapped tightly in a few sheets of plastic wrap.

Live

GIVE A JUST 'CUZ GIFT

I lo-o-o-o-ve surprises—whether I'm on the receiving or giving end. I play this card often, mainly because I love seeing people's eyes light up. No need to get fancy with it. No need to spend loads of money. In this instance, it's very true that the thought is what counts.

1 Biscuits and butter (see pages 21 and 58). I like to put my biscuits in wooden berry baskets I find at the craft store. A piece of linen and a nametag complete this gift.

2 A box of sugary kids' cereal and a pint of milk. No need to cute-ify this. The sight of a box of Fruit Loops will make your friend's heart leap.

3 Cheap supermarket flowers or a bundle of lavender (my neighborhood is full of bushes of this stuff) wrapped in brown craft paper. They look better this way.

4 Good cheese and a baguette. Bundle the two together with a long piece of raffia ribbon.

5 Your favorite soup and a baguette for dipping. I like to pour the soup into plastic quart-size deli containers. Be sure to add a simple note explaining the ingredients and how to reheat.

6 Dinner in a box (see page 29). Throwing everything in a cute tote bag makes this fuss free and adorable.

Do

SALT CELLAR

In the world of ceramics, most people are either hand-builders or throwers. I'm personally a thrower, not a fantastic one, but I do love it. From time to time, I do like to hand-build, and since I've been in search of a vessel to house my growing collection of black lava salt, smoked sea salt, and regular ol' sea salt and have come up short, I figured I'd make my own.

SUPPLIES

1½ pounds air-dry white clay

Waxed paper

Rolling pin

X-ACTO knife

Ruler or measuring tape

Small bowl of water

Watercolor paints

1   Place the clay on a sheet of waxed paper. Roll the clay, using your rolling pin, into an oblong shape that's about ⅛" thick.

2   Use the knife to cut out a rectangle that measures 12" long and 1½" wide; this piece will act as the wall. Set it aside.

3   Next, make the bottom of the salt cellar by rolling a second, smaller piece of clay into an oblong shape that's about ¼" thick. Cut a rectangle that measures 4" x 1½".

4   Place the long rectangle upright on top of the shorter rectangle, and wrap it around, creating 4 sides of the cellar. Reinforce the corners of the rectangle using your pointer finger.

(continued)

5 Create the 2 salt dividers by rolling out more clay to a ⅛" thickness and cutting out 1½" x 1½" squares. Insert them into the salt cellar. To keep them upright, place small clay balls on each side, pressing the balls into the foundation of the salt cellar.

6 To smooth out any cracks or shaggy bits on the piece, dip your finger into a bit of water and rub until smooth.

7 Carve an S in the front of the cellar, using your knife.

8 Allow to air-dry completely, about 2 days. Paint the sides of the salt cellar with the watercolor paint of your choice. Dry completely, about 3 hours, before filling with salts. Since there is no baking process, air-dry clay is fragile, so use it with a gentle hand.

BOMBOLONI WITH STRAWBERRY DIPLOMAT CREAM

March isn't the easiest of months. Spring begins to tease us, giving us warmer days and then throwing snow, sleet, and hail our way. These doughnuts, served with strawberry cream, are a way to anticipate spring without having to rely on its fresh fruit. They call for one of my favorite ingredients to bake and cook with: freeze-dried fruit. Freeze-dried fruit gives you all of the flavor without requiring the fruit to be fresh and without imparting juice, which isn't always welcome. The dough requires a slow overnight rise in the fridge, which requires some planning, but by the time you wake up, fresh warm doughnuts are minutes away. MAKES 22

BOMBOLONI

½ cup warm water

3¼ teaspoons active dry yeast

2 tablespoons honey

3 cups all-purpose flour, divided + additional for rolling

¼ cup whole milk

½ teaspoon grated lemon zest (from ½ lemon)

2 large eggs

2 egg yolks

¼ cup granulated sugar

1½ teaspoons sea salt

3 tablespoons unsalted butter, softened

4 cups canola oil + more for the bowl

Confectioners' sugar

1 *To make the bomboloni:* In the bowl of a stand mixer, add the warm water, yeast, honey, and 1 cup of the flour. Cover the bowl with plastic wrap and let it stand on the counter at room temperature until the mixture rises and becomes foamy, about 1 hour.

2 Place the bowl back on the mixer and fit it with the dough hook. Pour in the remaining 2 cups flour, milk, lemon zest, eggs, egg yolks, granulated sugar, and salt. Turn the mixer on low and mix until barely combined. Add the butter and continue mixing the dough for about 5 minutes, until it's sticky and smooth. Don't be concerned if the dough sticks to the sides of the bowl. Rub a little canola oil inside a clean, large bowl. Transfer the dough to the oiled bowl and cover it with plastic wrap. Place the dough in the fridge overnight. The dough will double in size.

3 *To make the strawberry diplomat cream:* While the dough is rising in the fridge, let's make the diplomat cream. In a food processor, pulse the strawberries until they turn powdery. They should measure about 2 tablespoons. Set aside.

(continued)

**¼ cup freeze-dried
strawberries**

**1 tablespoon all-purpose
flour**

1 tablespoon cornstarch

1 cup whole milk

**1 teaspoon pure vanilla
extract**

2 large egg yolks

**3 tablespoons granulated
sugar**

**2 drops red food coloring,
optional**

⅓ cup heavy cream

**1 tablespoon confectioners'
sugar**

4 In a small bowl, sift together the flour and cornstarch. In a small saucepan set over medium heat, combine the milk and vanilla and bring to a simmer, then immediately remove from the heat. In a medium bowl, whisk the egg yolks and granulated sugar until the mixture is a pale yellow. Add the flour mixture and whisk until completely smooth. While whisking the egg mixture, simultaneously add about half of the milk mixture to the bowl. Slowly adding the hot milk to the egg mixture will prevent the eggs from scrambling.

5 Transfer the egg/milk mixture back to the saucepan and place over medium-high heat. Add the freeze-dried strawberry powder. Bring to a simmer, whisking the entire time, being sure to scrape the bottom and the sides of the pan. Lower the heat and cook until the cream has thickened and hits 175°F, 2 to 3 minutes.

6 Remove the custard from the heat and pour it through a sieve into a bowl. This will eliminate any lumps and catch any strawberry bits. Stir in the food coloring, then press a piece of plastic wrap directly onto the custard's surface so it doesn't form a skin, and transfer it to the refrigerator to chill for 1 hour.

7 Combine the heavy cream and confectioners' sugar in a medium bowl. Using a hand mixer, beat until firm peaks form. Remove the chilled custard from the fridge and gently fold in the whipped cream. Return the diplomat cream to the refrigerator until you're ready to serve.

8 In a deep Dutch oven, heat the oil to 315°F. Line a plate with paper towels. On a lightly floured surface, roll out the dough to a ½" thickness. Using a 2" round or square biscuit cutter, stamp out the bomboloni. Drop into the hot oil and fry for about 4 minutes, or until they are golden brown, flipping them after the first 2 minutes. Keep the oil between 315°F and 330°F. If hotter, the bomboloni won't cook inside. Drain them on paper towels. Fry the remaining dough.

9 Immediately dust the bomboloni with confectioners' sugar and serve them warm alongside a ramekin of strawberry diplomat cream.

Spring

APRIL

GO ON A FOOD ADVENTURE AND EAT SOMETHING YOU'VE NEVER EATEN BEFORE

One of the perks about being with my boyfriend, who cooks in the restaurant industry, is his knack for finding adventurous eats. He believes that in order to cook well, you must eat well, too. This means he's constantly seeking out new food experiences. It's inspiring and fun, and it has made me a better cook. Eating different types of food is almost like traveling; it helps me understand other cultures and their stories, what's meaningful to them and why. It's educated me in ways a book simply cannot.

1 Do a bit of research. Jonathan Gold, a Pulitzer Prize–winning food journalist in Los Angeles, is a good source. We usually do a bit of googling and, sure enough, find that he's often covered the type of cuisine we're looking for. If we're traveling to another city, we usually go on Eater or Serious Eats or do some googling in search of a local blogger in that specific area.

2 Travel with cash since hole-in-the-wall-type restaurants tend not to accept credit cards.

3 Eat the specialty. I can't tell you how many times I've gone to a Korean restaurant and ordered the dish I was craving versus what that restaurant was known for. I've always regretted it. Many ethnic restaurants are good at one particular part of their culture's cuisine. Order that!

Make

FRUIT SUGARS

There's a little spice shop in my neighborhood of Silver Lake, and it has jars of the most beautifully colored sugars I ever laid eyes on. For years I've asked the people there how they made them. They threw up their hands, always telling me that they are purchased premade from a vendor. So, like the curious and somewhat neurotic person that I am, I bought all of them and took them home to examine up close.

I sprinkled them on baked goods: delicious! I put them on my cinnamon toast: tasty! But it wasn't until I put them in a cup of hot water that I learned the trick. I looked down and, as I stirred, I noticed little particles separating from the sugar granules. Aha! The sugar was coated in powdered freeze-dried fruit. So I tried it . . . and, you guys, it worked. It really worked! The trick is to add a teeny bit of water to bind the powdered freeze-dried fruit to the sugar. A few hours later, after you spread the stuff out on a baking sheet to dry, you'll be on your way to making naturally flavored and colored sugars. They make gorgeous, super-inexpensive gifts. They're good in a cup of tea or coffee or on baked goods. MAKES 1 CUP

½ cup freeze-dried fruit (peaches, pineapples, blueberries, or strawberries)

1 cup pure cane sugar

⅛ teaspoon water

1 In a blender or food processor, place the freeze-dried fruit. Pulse until the mixture resembles a powder. If some bits are stubborn, set them aside, and pulse the large bits once more.

2 In a bowl, combine the powdered freeze-dried fruit and the sugar. Add the water. Rub the entire mixture vigorously with your hands until the sugar turns the corresponding color.

3 Transfer the sugar to a parchment-lined baking sheet and spread it out to dry. Place the baking sheet near a sunny window to dry for 1 to 2 hours.

Blueberry

Pineapple

Strawberry

Peach

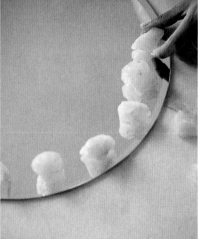  

Do

GEM TRAY

My friend Lara is the quartz queen. She paints quartz crystals using mineral paint, and, really, it's her fault that I'm obsessed with them as much as I am. While I'm uncertain about their energy qualities, I do know that I love the beauty they bring to my tables. I decided to combine my obsession for pretty rose quartz with the need to house my ever-growing liquor collection. Instead of finding a tray to glue them to, I opted for a really inexpensive round mirror I found at the craft store.

SUPPLIES

12" round mirror

No-slip pads (optional)

10 (1") rose quartz crystals (approximately 1 pound)

Super Glue

Shopping Tips: I found my mirror at Michaels craft store and a pound of rose quartz crystals on Amazon.com.

1 My mirror came with no-slip pads on the bottom; if yours doesn't, I'd advise buying some and spacing them about 1" from the edges and a few inches from each other. This will keep the mirror from moving all over the place when you use it as a tray.

2 Arrange the rose quartz crystals around the mirror, leaving about a ¼" space around the edges. Carefully add the glue to the flattest side of a crystal. Stick it on the mirror and hold it firmly to the surface for about 30 seconds. Repeat this process with each of the crystals until you've gone all the way around the mirror. Allow to dry, undisturbed, for at least 24 hours.

3 There's a good chance your fingerprints are now all over the mirror. Give the mirror a clean with a paper towel and some window cleaner. Arrange your favorite liquors on top.

Live

EMBRACE YOUR INNER CHILD

Being a grown-up is intense. There are taxes, bills, responsibilities, people who depend on me, thoughts about my future, and—really, the list goes on and on. Some days it feels as if the weight of the world is upon my shoulders. For me, acting silly, laughing, and letting loose helps. Lucky for me, the neighborhood kids built a swing near my house. They've drawn cute stick figures on it and even put tassels on the rope. Whenever I'm feeling like life is too weighty, I swing as high as I can. It reminds me that it's all going to be okay.

Other adventures that make me wide-eyed and hopeful are:

1 Going to a roller rink, drinking lots of soda, and skating to Beyoncé.

2 Building a fort in my living room. Amelia thinks it's the most fun thing in the world to hide under bedsheets.

3 Having a pillow fight. Seriously. Try it.

4 Playing a good-natured practical joke on someone.

5 Challenging your friend to a race.

Do

FOOD-INSPIRED FLOWER ARRANGEMENT

The flowers that belong to some of my favorite foods are really beautiful. For years I often wondered why we don't include them in flower arrangements. Artichoke flowers? Beautiful. Broccoli flowers? Dainty, and they taste just like broccoli! And even enoki mushrooms can be strangely stunning. I always try to include at least one food element in my flower arrangements—it gives new meaning to the phrase "edible arrangement."

SUPPLIES

Pruning shears

Vase

1 bunch clover

1 artichoke

1 bunch ornamental kale

1 bunch Queen Anne's lace

Fresh mint sprigs

1 I like to select flowers with different thicknesses and heights. In this case I went with skinny clovers, a short and stout artichoke, round ornamental kale, fresh and white Queen Anne's lace, and mint sprigs as filler.

2 Place the largest flower at the very front of the vase and position it to one side. Start building the layers. I say get creative with it! I tend to position flowers so they arch out of the vase to the right or left side.

3 Finish by adding the white Queen Anne's lace in places where volume is needed. Since mint sprigs tend to be on the shorter side, I think they're perfect to cover the base of the arrangement. Be sure to place them all the way around.

Make

HOMEMADE GOAT CHEESE

Making my own cheese feels so fancy. I want you to feel fancy, too! Goat cheese is simple. It can be made with lemon juice and a bit of salt. How is this different than store-bought goat cheese? I'd say it's creamier and less dense than what I've purchased at the grocery store. Plus, when you make it at home, you can add whatever you want. I love folding in a bit of fresh herbs and then putting this cheese on everything I can get my hands on. And don't throw out the whey! You can use it to replace the buttermilk in my favorite biscuit recipe ever, Flaky, Buttery Biscuits (page 21). **MAKES ½ CUP**

1 quart fresh goat's milk

6 tablespoons lemon juice (from about 2 large lemons)

1 teaspoon salt

Tip: Fresh goat's milk can oftentimes be found at your local farmers' market or Trader Joe's or Whole Foods Market.

1 Place a medium saucepan over medium heat and add the goat's milk. Heat the milk to 180°F and then immediately remove it from the heat and mix in the lemon juice and salt. Allow the mixture to sit for 5 minutes, until the goat's milk slowly begins to coagulate.

2 Line a sieve with 4 to 5 layers of cheesecloth and place the sieve over a large bowl. Slowly pour the goat's milk mixture into the cheesecloth. If too much whey begins to gather on the bottom of the bowl, dump it out so the cheesecloth isn't sitting in the whey. Drain for 1 to 2 hours.

3 Gather the cheese in the cheesecloth and lightly squeeze it so any extra moisture drains out.

I love this goat cheese by itself, slathered on a piece of bread, but if you'd like to make it a bit more interesting, here are some good ideas.

LAVENDER-HONEY GOAT CHEESE: After the cheese is made, immediately fold in a teaspoon of fresh lavender and a tablespoon of honey.

HERBED GOAT CHEESE: After the cheese is made, immediately fold in 2 tablespoons of finely chopped fresh dill, chives, or flat-leaf parsley.

GOAT CHEESE GNOCCHI

I like gnocchi to taste like little clouds of fluffy potatoes that a cherub would crave. To achieve the lightness I'm after, I opt to use no eggs, which is sort of controversial. (If your Italian grandmother makes gnocchi with egg yolks and you hate me right now, I understand, I really do.) Regardless of which side of the yolk debate you stand on, I think we can all agree that goat cheese makes everything better. The watercress, with its jab of spice, and the freshness from blistered favas make this dish very, for lack of a better word, spring-y. **SERVES 4**

GNOCCHI

1 pound russet potatoes (about 2)

1½ tablespoons goat cheese, store-bought or homemade (opposite)

Salt

¼–½ cup all-purpose flour + additional if needed

Olive oil

BROTH

2 cups vegetable broth

2 tablespoons heavy cream

Salt

Ground black pepper

Juice from ½ lemon

1 teaspoon + 1 tablespoon olive oil

1 cup watercress, stems trimmed

½ pound fava beans, shelled

1 *To make the gnocchi:* Preheat the oven to 400°F. Place the potatoes on a baking sheet and bake until they're tender when poked with a fork, about 1 hour. When the potatoes are done, immediately slice them open to let the steam out.

2 Scoop the potato flesh into a potato ricer. Push all of the potato through the ricer and into a bowl. (The riced potato should equal 2 cups.) Add the goat cheese to the center of the potatoes. Sprinkle with ¼ teaspoon salt or more, according to taste. Meanwhile, bring a large pot of water to a boil. Add a few pinches of salt.

3 Sprinkle ¼ cup of the flour onto your clean counter or cutting board. Knead the potatoes with it, sprinkling in another ¼ cup flour, until the dough just comes together. If it's still pretty shaggy, add more flour, 1 tablespoon at a time.

4 Now for the test! Pinch off a piece of dough and roll it out into a tube. Cut it into a few pieces and drop them into the boiling water to make sure they hold their shape. If they fall apart in the water, knead the dough a bit more. When kneaded just right, the gnocchi will float to the top and look a little ragged, but they should hold together.

(continued)

5 Line a baking sheet with parchment paper. Roll the rest of the dough into ropes that are about ½" thick, then cut the ropes into ½" lengths. Transfer the gnocchi to the baking sheet, being sure the gnocchi don't touch each other. You should have about 40 gnocchi.

6 Add the gnocchi to the large pot of boiling water in batches of about 10. Adjust the heat so the water doesn't reach a rolling boil—it should be more like an aggressive simmer. When the gnocchi rise to the surface of the water, they're done. Remove them with a slotted spoon or mesh strainer and transfer them to a paper towel. Drizzle the gnocchi with a teeny bit of olive oil—this will prevent them from sticking to one another as they sit.

7 *To make the broth:* The end of this dish goes very quickly. In a medium saucepan, bring the vegetable broth and heavy cream to a light simmer. Season to taste with salt and pepper. Bring the heat down to low so the broth stays hot while you prepare the rest of the dish.

8 In a small bowl, whisk together the lemon juice and 1 teaspoon oil. Add the watercress and toss until the leaves are thoroughly coated. Add a few pinches of salt and massage the leaves once more.

9 Add the remaining 1 tablespoon oil to a small nonstick skillet set over medium heat. When the oil is hot and glistens, add the favas. Cook them, shaking the skillet every so often to avoid sticking, until they're blistered. Remove them from the heat and sprinkle them with a teeny pinch of salt. If you like, you can sear the gnocchi on both sides for about 1 minute.

10 *To assemble the dish:* Divide the gnocchi among 4 bowls, about 10 pieces per person (this can vary depending on how hungry you are). Ladle the warm broth over the gnocchi, sprinkle in the favas, and add a mound of watercress to the very center.

Live

MAKE A WISH

1 Make a wish on a cake.

2 Make a wish on the florets of a dandelion.

3 Make a wish on the snap of a wishbone. Cross your fingers in hopes that you get the larger part of the wishbone.

4 Make a wish on a fallen eyelash.

5 Make a wish on a sunset.

It could come true.

MAY

Make

BAKED COCONUT-LEMON DOUGHNUTS

In all my days, I have never met anyone who doesn't like doughnuts. People dislike pie, cake, and ice cream, but never doughnuts. These doughnuts are of the baked variety. The flavors are bright, fresh, and tropical, and they make you feel like summer is just around the corner.

MAKES 1 DOZEN

DOUGHNUTS

¾ cup cake flour

½ cup + 1 tablespoon granulated sugar

½ teaspoon baking powder

¼ teaspoon baking soda

½ teaspoon salt

3 large egg yolks

¼ cup coconut oil, melted and cooled slightly

¼ cup water

3 tablespoons grated lemon zest (from 3 lemons)

1 tablespoon + 1 teaspoon lemon juice

1 teaspoon pure vanilla extract

3 large egg whites

¼ cup shredded unsweetened coconut

GLAZE

3 cups confectioners' sugar, sifted

6 tablespoons lemon juice

Pinch of salt

1 **To make the doughnuts:** Preheat the oven to 325°F. In a medium bowl, mix together the cake flour, ½ cup granulated sugar, baking powder, baking soda, and salt.

2 In a large bowl, whisk together the egg yolks, oil, water, lemon zest, 1 tablespoon lemon juice, and vanilla. In 2 batches, add the flour mixture to the coconut-lemon mixture until just combined.

3 In another medium bowl, combine the egg whites, 1 teaspoon lemon juice, and 1 tablespoon granulated sugar. Using a hand mixer with the whisk attachment, beat the egg whites until medium to stiff peaks form, about 5 to 7 minutes. Gently fold the beaten egg whites into the batter until completely combined. Add the coconut and mix one last time.

4 Liberally coat your doughnut pan with cooking spray and spoon the batter into each cavity, filling it about three-quarters of the way full. Bake for 10 to 12 minutes, or until the doughnuts are golden brown and spring back when touched.

5 Allow the doughnuts to cool completely in the pan on a cooling rack before running a butter knife around the edges to release them. Repeat the process with the remaining batter.

6 **To make the glaze:** In a medium bowl, whisk together the confectioners' sugar, lemon juice, and salt. Dip the cooled doughnuts into the glaze and transfer back to the cooling rack for the glaze to set.

NASTURTIUM BUCATINI

Is there a dish your mom used to make for you when everything was wrong in the world? This dish probably involved sugar, carbs, and/or butter. Most likely it felt like comfort in a bowl—a mom hug in the form of food. My mom would make me tallarines verde, a Peruvian dish that translates literally to "green spaghetti." This recipe is an extension of that idea using nasturtium, a spicy watercress that grows in abundance on the sides of roads, in fields, and up hills. The leaves are spicy and grassy and when paired with queso blanco (a salty fresh cheese from South America) and pasta, it will feel like home. Don't forget to pick the flowers, which will be in full bloom March through May. **MAKES 4 SERVINGS**

¼ cup canola or grape seed oil

¼ cup water

1 garlic clove, peeled

2 cups packed nasturtium leaves, stems trimmed and discarded

8 ounces queso blanco or queso fresco, cubed

½ teaspoon salt, or to taste

1 pound bucatini or spaghetti

1 To a blender, add the oil, water, garlic, nasturtium leaves, and queso blanco or queso fresco. Pulse until smooth, about 30 seconds to 1 minute. Add the salt, pulse one last time, and give it a taste. Adjust the salt to your liking. Set aside.

2 Bring a medium pot of salted water to a boil. Add the bucatini or spaghetti and cook until al dente, usually about 10 minutes, but be sure to reference the back of the package since each batch is slightly different. Drain the pasta, reserving about ¼ cup of pasta water, and immediately return the pasta to the pot. Add the nasturtium pesto and toss until thoroughly coated, adding a splash or two of pasta water if needed. Transfer the pasta to a serving plate and garnish with a few nasturtium flowers.

Note: Queso blanco or queso fresco can usually be found at South American markets. I also find that Whole Foods has it most of the time, too.

Note: Be sure to forage for the leaves in areas you know aren't being sprayed with pesticides or any fake fertilizers. In Los Angeles, I find that nasturtium growing on the hillsides is perfect to pick.

BREAKFAST IN BED

I'd be lying if I said I have breakfast in bed all the time. This isn't a magazine, this is real life! It's not the most realistic of places to eat a whole meal, especially when you have a food-begging corgi like I do. But whenever I take the time to make up a tray all nice and break out the waffle maker, it feels so fun and special.

Here are some sort-of-spillproof breakfast-in-bed options.

1   Belgian waffles

2   A stack of fluffy pancakes

3   A slice of frittata

4   An acai bowl

5   Baked eggs with wilted kale and toast

Do

HOMEMADE ROSE PETAL LIP BALM

I'm not a big lipstick girl. I'm usually eating and drinking way too much to keep up with the maintenance of the "perfect lips." Instead, my allegiance lies with lip balm. I usually have at least a few different versions in my purse. My preference is for a little color just because if I don't have any color at all, I look like I'm sickly, and I like my lip balm to be refreshing— a little tingle is nice! Since I'm a teeny bit picky about my lip balm, I like to make my own. It's easily customizable (I like to make mine extra tingly!), and I find making it a lot less expensive than buying it at Sephora. Also, I love making a big batch and giving the extras to my friends. MAKES 8 LIP BALMS

SUPPLIES
2 tablespoons beeswax pellets

1 tablespoon coconut oil

1 drop tea tree oil

1 drop rose essential oil

1 piece (¼") cheap drugstore lipstick (optional)

Wooden craft stick or skewer

8 (2-ounce) plastic lip balm containers

Dried rose petals

1 In a makeshift double boiler (I like to use a glass measuring cup set in a pot holding a few inches of water), place the beeswax pellets, coconut oil, tea tree oil, rose oil, and piece of lipstick, if using.

2 Heat over medium heat until the beeswax pellets are completely dissolved. I like using a disposable wooden craft stick to stir the lip balm together, but a wooden skewer will also work.

3 Fill the lip balm containers about halfway. Sprinkle a few pinches of dried rose petals into the lip balm and then top with the remaining lip balm liquid and a few more pinches of rose petals.

4 Allow to cool completely and to set, about 2 hours.

Tips: The beeswax pellets can be found online. I love buying small containers of essential oils from Whole Foods or my local health food store. Feel free to swap in different oils depending on your preference. The cheap drugstore lipstick addition is completely optional, though I do love the hint of color it gives. The 2-ounce lip balm containers can be found in the travel section at The Container Store.

Make

BLOODY MARY BAR

I'm not a big fan of going out for brunch. The long wait times, the crowds, the slow service are all amplified by the fact that I'm usually a lil' hungover and a lot hungry, so I feel like I might be flirting with death. Drama. So that's why I usually opt for brunch at my house. Bloody Mary bars are the way to people's hungover hearts on a Sunday morning. Since many people are particular about their Bloody Marys (including me), I like making a good and somewhat neutral mix and then allowing people to customize their own. The additions might be the most important part. I like my Bloody Mary to be one part drink, one part snack. Have you ever met another drink that is a vessel for snacks? Me neither, and that's why I love them so.

MAKES 8 TO 10 SERVINGS

(continued)

BLOODY MARY MIX

4 ribs celery, chopped

Juice from 1 lemon

1 jar (32 ounces) tomato juice

½ teaspoon celery salt

1 tablespoon fresh horseradish

1 tablespoon Worcestershire sauce

3–4 teaspoons hot sauce (to taste)

½ teaspoon ground black pepper

¼ cup stout beer

ADDITIONS

Pepperoni sticks

Celery ribs

Green olives

Lemon and lime wedges

Cornichons

Bacon pieces

Boiled shrimp

Blue cheese cubes

Hot sauce

Worcestershire sauce

Gin

Vodka

1 *To make the Bloody Mary mix:* In a blender, puree the celery and lemon juice until the mixture resembles a slushy from 7-Eleven. Pour the puree through a strainer into a bowl. You should end up with ⅓ cup of celery juice. Alternatively, if you own a juicer, you can juice the celery.

2 In a large pitcher, combine the celery juice, tomato juice, celery salt, horseradish, Worcestershire sauce, hot sauce, and black pepper. Transfer to the refrigerator to chill for at least 1 hour, or ideally overnight. Right before serving, mix in the stout beer.

3 *To prepare the additions:* Fill up a bevy of small bowls, ramekins, and cups with the pepperoni sticks, celery ribs, green olives, lemon and lime wedges, cornichons, bacon pieces, shrimp, and blue cheese cubes. Set out bottles of hot sauce and Worcestershire so people can add more if they like and 2 bottles of booze: gin and vodka. I prefer my Bloody Mary with gin—the juniper berries add the best flavor.

Make

PAN-ROASTED BRANZINO WITH CHERRY TOMATOES AND QUINOA

Eating a whole fish reminds me of my papa. We'd go to our neighborhood Colombian restaurant, just the two of us, and order a whole fried fish. Nothing made him happier than seeing me eat it. Even though the fish's eyeballs staring back at me sort of freaked me out, I loved every last bite.

There's something really dramatic and beautiful about serving a whole fish. It feels like a bit of a grand gesture. The good news is that it isn't all that labor intensive, especially since this preparation, unlike the one from my childhood, doesn't involve deep-frying. This dish is intended to be served family-style, with a few plates on the side and glasses filled with chilled wine. I initially intended it to be for a celebration of sorts, like Mother's Day or a spring brunch, but the more I made this dish, the more I realized that it's actually fairly quick and totally suitable for a normal Wednesday night dinner. SERVES 2 OR 3

¼ cup quinoa

¾ cup water

Salt

1 large branzino or 2 small branzini (about 1 pound), scaled, gutted, and cleaned (see note on page 154)

4–5 tablespoons olive oil, divided

1 pint cherry tomatoes, halved

¼ pound sugar snap peas, shucked

Small handful of coarsely chopped Italian parsley

2–3 leaves mint, finely chopped

Juice from ½ lemon

3 tablespoons unsalted butter

1   Place the quinoa in a fine-mesh strainer and rinse under cold water. Transfer the quinoa, along with the ¾ cup water, to a small saucepan over medium heat. Mix in ¼ teaspoon of salt. When the quinoa mixture reaches a rolling boil, turn the heat down to low and cover the pan. Cook the quinoa for 12 to 15 minutes, until it has bloomed and the water has evaporated.

2   Preheat the oven to 400°F. Sprinkle the fish on both sides and the inside with a few pinches of salt. In a large cast-iron skillet or ovenproof sauté pan over medium-high heat, heat a few tablespoons of oil. When the oil is very hot, add the branzino. Sear the first side for 1 to 2 minutes, or until very crisp. Flip and cook the opposite side for an additional 1 to 2 minutes. Transfer the skillet to the oven and roast for 5 minutes, or until the fish is tender to the touch.

(continued)

3 Meanwhile, in a saucepan over medium-high heat, heat 2 tablespoons of oil. When the oil is hot, add the tomatoes. Cook the tomatoes until the skins are slightly blistered and the juices have released, about 2 minutes. Add the snap peas, parsley, and mint and cook for an additional 2 minutes. Turn the heat to medium-low and add the lemon juice, butter, and a teaspoon of salt. Toss everything together until the butter has melted.

4 Transfer the quinoa to the center of a large serving dish. Place the branzino atop the quinoa and pour the pea and tomato mixture on top. Serve the fish family-style.

Note: Be sure to ask your fishmonger to scale, gut, and clean the branzino.

PLANT AN HERB GARDEN

I wasn't born with a green thumb. In fact, keeping all my plants alive is a daily struggle. It's not in my nature to think about their needs, and I blame this on my mother. She doesn't have a green thumb either. In fact, one of my fondest memories of her is looking on as a kid while she rubbed mayonnaise on her plant's leaves because she "read it in a magazine." Needless to say, the plant didn't think the mayonnaise was delicious and died a few days later.

The conundrum here is that I love having fresh herbs in my house. Very rarely do I use a whole package from the store; so many times my store-bought herbs end up withering away and I'm forced to throw them out—what a waste! Growing my own herbs means I can clip off what I need and I always have fresh herbs in my house.

Options for an herb garden:

1 If you have the room outside, whether in the backyard or on a deck, you can buy a wooden planter. Be sure to plant the herbs about 12 inches apart. This gives them room to grow.

2 If you're an apartment dweller like me, with no outside area of your own, you can dedicate a windowsill to housing various herbs. Pick ones that you cook with the most. For me, it's thyme, rosemary, mint, and basil. I like to replant them with a bit of potting soil in old (but clean!) San Marzano tomato cans. Be sure to drill a hole in the bottom so they can drain.

DIP-DYED DOG'S LEASH

There's nothing ladylike about Amelia. She burps after every meal, she loves nothing more than rolling around in the mud, and she happily eats old, moldy slices of pizza she finds in the tall grass at the park. But that doesn't mean I don't want her leash to be as pretty as possible. After scouring the Internet and balking at the price for a stylish dog leash, I figured I could simply make my own. I ordered a very inexpensive horse lead rope, dip-dyed it, added a few pieces of suede twine, and my goal of achieving adorableness was met.

SUPPLIES

Rubber gloves

5-quart plastic bucket

3½ quarts warm water

1 packet (1⅛ ounces) powdered dye

6' white cotton lead rope with solid brass snap

Suede twine (about 1')

Fabric glue (optional)

Tip: The horse lead rope with solid brass snap can be found at most animal supply stores (just make sure they have a horse section). You can also find the lead rope online.

1 Put on your gloves. Fill the bucket with the warm water. Mix in ¼ teaspoon of the powdered dye. Take the first end of the rope and dip about 2 feet of it into the dye. Count to 20 and then remove the rope from the dye. Repeat with the other end of the rope. Ideally, you'll leave a gap in the center of the rope completely white.

2 Mix another ¼ teaspoon of powdered dye into the water. Repeat the process of dipping the rope, but this time don't go as high. Repeat until you've reached the ends of the rope. Allow the very ends to soak for 1 minute in the dye, as we want these to be the darkest parts of the rope. Allow the rope to air-dry completely, which will take at least 4 hours but most likely overnight.

3 Wrap the suede twine around the shaggy parts of the rope (a horse's lead rope generally has 2 places that need covering). Secure the suede twine by tying it or by applying a dot of fabric glue onto the rope, if desired.

Burnt Cherry
and Vanilla Pie

Classic
Peach Pie

Blackberry-Walnut
Crumble Pie

Make

SUMMER PIES

Pies, oh, pies! Pies aren't just pies, are they? Between their layers of flakiness and pockets of sweet, ripe fruit is so much more. Pie recipes can be family heirlooms; pies can be a symbol of your love and courage and faith; they can accompany you to a party and work their magical charm, even if you're awkward and tell badly timed jokes; and the process of making a pie can help you work your way through a broken heart—it's been proven.

If you've never made a pie, you might be a little stressed at some point. They're not the easiest dessert to make, but man, if you master making pies, you will feel like the baddest chick/dude on the planet. Like most good things in life, making a pie takes a little bit of practice. If you can't make a perfect crimp at first try, don't stress—just present it to your friends and put the word "rustic" in front of its name. Example: "You guys, look at my beautiful *rustic* Blackberry–Walnut Crumble Pie!" And then put a big ol' scoop of ice cream right on top of each slice. Trust me, after that, no one will care.

I have some very strong opinions about pie. First, I don't believe in large amounts of sugar. If you're using ripe fruit, its sugars will come out. And I believe a good salty and buttery crust is the necessary backdrop for tart fruit. None of these pies is overly complicated with flavors that compete. Instead, there's one element, oftentimes savory, that blends perfectly with the sweetness.

BLACKBERRY-WALNUT CRUMBLE PIE

This pie is a mash-up of your favorite blackberry pie and a bubbly fruit crumble. The walnuts add a much-needed texture, while the fall spices, like cardamom and cinnamon, work wonderfully with the ripe summer blackberries. MAKES ONE 9" PIE

SINGLE PIECRUST

1¾ cups all-purpose flour + additional for working

2 teaspoons sugar

¾ teaspoon fine-grain sea salt

½ cup unsalted butter, frozen

¼ cup + 2–3 tablespoons very cold water

FILLING

3½ pints blackberries (about 5 cups)

½ cup sugar

¼ cup tapioca flour

1 teaspoon salt

¾ teaspoon ground cardamom

½ teaspoon ground cinnamon

1   **To make the piecrust:** In a large bowl, mix together the flour, sugar, and salt. Using a box grater, grate the cold butter atop the flour mixture. Working quickly and using your hands, break the butter bits into the flour until they're evenly distributed and the size of small peas.

2   Add ¼ cup of the water and mix. Using your hands, dig in the bowl and knead the dough 3 to 5 times; you'll notice it will begin to come together. If the mixture is still shaggy, add a tablespoon of water at a time until it comes together. Flour your counter or work surface and dump the dough onto it. Knead the dough a few more times and form it into a 1"-thick disk. Wrap the dough in plastic wrap and transfer it to the refrigerator to chill for at least 1½ hours, or ideally overnight.

3   When the dough is done resting, remove it from the fridge and allow it to shake off its chill for 10 minutes (this will make it easier to roll out). Liberally flour your work surface and rolling pin. Begin to roll out the dough to a 13" round that's about ⅛" thick, being sure to rotate it every so often to avoid sticking. Wrap the dough around the rolling pin and unroll it over a 9" pie dish. Gently fit the dough into the bottom and up the sides of the pie dish. Trim the edge, leaving a 1" overhang, and tuck the overhang under itself. To make a crimp pattern, set your thumb on the outside edge of the crust. With your opposite pointer finger and thumb, create a V, then push together from both directions. Repeat this process all the way around the piecrust. Transfer the piecrust to the freezer to chill for 30 minutes.

½ cup all-purpose flour

¼ cup unsalted butter, chilled

½ cup chopped walnuts

3 tablespoons sugar

Pinch of salt

½ cup old-fashioned oats or rye flakes

1 large egg, beaten

4 *To make the filling:* In a medium bowl, mix together the blackberries, sugar, tapioca flour, salt, cardamom, and cinnamon.

5 *To make the topping:* Add the flour to a small bowl. Using a box grater, grate in the cold butter and mix until evenly distributed. Add the walnuts, sugar, salt, and oats or rye flakes and mix. Preheat the oven to 400°F.

6 *To assemble the pie:* Remove the crust from the freezer. Pour in the filling and top the pie with the crumble mixture. Brush the crimped edges with the beaten egg. Transfer the pie to a baking sheet and bake for 30 to 40 minutes, or until the piecrust is golden brown and the blackberries are bubbling. If at any time the edges of the piecrust turn a bit too dark, tent the edges with a sheet of foil.

7 Allow the pie to cool for at least 3 hours before cutting. This will ensure that it doesn't spill all over the place, but worse things have happened, right? So dig in immediately, if you must.

CLASSIC PEACH PIE

This peach pie is like a perfect-fitting white T-shirt or pair of jeans. There isn't anything exotic, unusual, or different about this pie. It doesn't call for a weird combination of ingredients or out-of-the-ordinary technique; instead, it relies on perfect ratios of sugar to fruit to bourbon, giving you a perfect classic peach pie experience. **MAKES ONE 9" PIE**

DOUBLE PIECRUST

2½ cups all-purpose flour + additional for working

1 tablespoon granulated sugar

1½ teaspoons fine-grain sea salt

1 cup unsalted butter, frozen

¾ cup very cold water, divided

1 *To make the piecrust:* In a large bowl, mix together the flour, sugar, and salt. Using a box grater, grate the cold butter atop the flour mixture. Working quickly and using your hands, break the butter bits into the flour until evenly distributed and the size of small peas.

2 Add ½ cup of the water and mix. Using your hands, dig in the bowl and knead the dough 3 to 5 times; you'll notice it will begin to come together. If the mixture is still shaggy, add a tablespoon of water at a time until it comes together. Flour your counter or work surface and dump the dough onto it. Knead the dough a few more times and form it into a ball. Cut the ball in half, and form each half into a 1"-thick disk. Wrap each disk with plastic wrap, and transfer to the refrigerator to chill for at least 1½ hours, or ideally overnight.

3 When the dough is done resting, remove the first disk from the fridge and allow it to shake off its chill for 10 minutes (this will make it easier to roll out). Liberally flour your work surface and rolling pin. Begin to roll out the dough to a 13" round that's about ⅛" thick, being sure to rotate it every so often to avoid sticking. Wrap the dough around the rolling pin and unroll it over a 9" pie dish. Gently fit the dough into the bottom and up the sides of the pie dish and trim, leaving a 1" overhang. Transfer the piecrust to the freezer to chill for 30 minutes while you make the filling.

(continued)

FILLING

5–6 firm yet ripe yellow peaches, sliced (2 pounds)

¼ cup granulated sugar

¼ cup light brown sugar

4 tablespoons tapioca flour

2 tablespoons bourbon

1 teaspoon freshly grated ginger

Juice from ½ lemon

½ teaspoon salt

1 large egg, beaten

1 teaspoon turbinado sugar (optional)

4 **To make the filling:** In a large bowl, combine the peaches, sugars, tapioca flour, bourbon, ginger, lemon, and salt. Mix until the peaches are completely coated.

5 **To assemble the pie:** Remove the piecrust from the freezer and pour in the filling. Take the second disk of pie dough from the fridge, allow it to sit at room temperature for 10 minutes, and roll it out to another 13" round that's about ⅛" thick. At this time you have some options. You can cut the dough into strips for a lattice top, cut out small circles using a piping tip for a polka-dot effect, or simply lay the dough on top of the pie and make slits on the top. Whatever top you choose, be sure to seal the top crust to the bottom by trimming the overhang and crimping the top and bottom crusts together. Be sure to cut a vent to let out the steam. Transfer the entire assembled pie to the freezer and chill for 15 minutes. Meanwhile, preheat the oven to 425°F.

6 Brush the crust with the beaten egg, sprinkle with turbinado sugar (if using), and place the pie on a baking sheet. Bake for 25 minutes. Turn the heat down to 350°F and bake for an additional 30 minutes, or until the filling is bubbling and the crust is golden brown. If at any time the edges of the piecrust turn a bit too dark, tent the edges with a sheet of foil.

7 Allow the pie to cool completely before slicing, 3 to 4 hours.

BURNT CHERRY AND VANILLA PIE

The flavor profile of "burnt" can be delightful. I know this may seem strange, but I love the char on steak, and a piece of slightly burnt toast is my favorite. In this case, charred vanilla bean and blistered cherries offer an interesting and delicious departure from your usual cherry pie.

MAKES ONE 9" PIE

DOUBLE PIECRUST

2½ cups all-purpose flour + additional for working

1 tablespoon sugar

1½ teaspoons fine-grain sea salt

1 cup unsalted butter, frozen

¾ cup very cold water, divided

FILLING

1 vanilla bean

½ cup sugar

2 pounds cherries, pitted and halved

¼ cup tapioca flour

½ teaspoon salt

1 large egg, beaten

1 teaspoon turbinado sugar (optional)

1 *To make the piecrust:* In a large bowl, mix together the flour, sugar, and salt. Using a box grater, grate the cold butter atop the flour mixture. Working quickly and using your hands, break the butter bits into the flour until they are evenly distributed and the size of small peas.

2 Add ½ cup of the water and mix. Using your hands, dig in the bowl and knead the dough 3 to 5 times; you'll notice it will begin to come together. If the mixture is still shaggy, add a tablespoon of water at a time until it comes together. Flour your counter or work surface and dump the dough onto it. Knead the dough a few more times and form it into a ball. Cut the ball in half, and form each half into a 1"-thick disk. Wrap each disk with plastic wrap and transfer it to the refrigerator to chill for at least 1½ hours, or ideally overnight.

3 When the dough is done resting, remove the first disk from the fridge and allow it to shake off its chill for 10 minutes (this will make it easier to roll out). Liberally flour your work surface and rolling pin. Begin to roll out the dough to a 13" round that's about ⅛" thick, being sure to rotate it every so often to avoid sticking. Wrap the dough around the rolling pin and unroll it over a 9" pie dish. Gently fit the dough into the bottom and up the sides of the pie dish, leaving a 1" overhang. Transfer the piecrust to the refrigerator to chill for 30 minutes while you make the filling.

(continued)

4 *To make the filling:* Over the grate of a gas stove burner set on medium heat, carefully rotate the vanilla bean until both sides are charred. Allow it to cool completely. Pulse the burnt vanilla bean in a food processor until it resembles a powder. Add the sugar and pulse once more until the vanilla bean is thoroughly distributed throughout.

5 Preheat the broiler. In a medium ovenproof skillet or a foil-lined baking sheet, place the cherries skin-side up (you may need to do this in batches). Broil for 5 minutes, watching them the entire time, or until the skins are blistered and slightly charred and the cherries are juicy. Transfer the cherries, their juices, and the vanilla bean sugar to a bowl. Add the tapioca flour and salt. Mix until combined.

6 *To assemble the pie:* Remove the pie dish from the refrigerator and pour in the filling. Remove the second disk of pie dough from the fridge, allow it to sit at room temperature for 10 minutes, and roll it out to another 13" round that's about $\frac{1}{8}$" thick. At this time you have some options. You can cut the dough into strips for a lattice top, cut out small circles using a piping tip for a polka-dot effect, or simply lay the dough on top of the pie and make slits on the top. Whatever top you choose, be sure to seal the top crust to the bottom by trimming the overhang and crimping the top and bottom crusts together. Transfer the entire assembled pie to the freezer and chill for 15 minutes. Meanwhile, preheat the oven to 425°F.

7 Brush the piecrust with the beaten egg, sprinkle with turbinado sugar (if using), and place the pie on a baking sheet. Bake for 30 minutes. Turn the heat down to 350°F and bake for an additional 15 to 30 minutes. You'll know the pie is done when the cherry juice is bubbling and the crust is golden brown. I always recommend checking on it periodically. If at any time the piecrust begins to get too dark, create a foil tent to protect it.

8 Allow to cool completely before slicing, 3 to 4 hours.

Make

AGUAS FRESCAS

When I first moved to Los Angeles, I had no idea what aguas frescas were, but once I saw them, I knew I wanted all of them. Aguas frescas are typically made with fresh summer fruit, pureed and mixed with water and, in some cases, sugar. They're a beautiful sight when lined up side by side. The Cantaloupe Agua Fresca recipe (page 170) uses the fruit's seeds and flesh, which many say adds a hint of almond flavor. The watermelon version (page 171) might be my all-time favorite because it's just so dang refreshing. And if you get a good watermelon, you'll need no sugar at all. If you're looking for an iced tea with a bit of tartness, go with the Agua de Jamaica (page 171) —it's fragrant and it will certainly quench your thirst.

(continued)

Watermelon
Agua Fresca

Cantaloupe
Agua Fresca

Agua de
Jamaica

CANTALOUPE AGUA FRESCA

MAKES 4 CUPS

1 cantaloupe (about 4 pounds), flesh and seeds scooped out

2 cups water, divided

2 tablespoons pure cane sugar + additional, if needed

Juice from ½ lime

1 In a blender, place the cantaloupe flesh, its seeds, ½ cup of the water, the 2 tablespoons of sugar, and the lime juice. (You may need to do this in batches, depending on the size of your blender.) Pulse until completely smooth and pureed, about 1 minute.

2 Line a strainer with cheesecloth and set it over a bowl. Pour the mixture through, allowing it to slowly drain for about 20 minutes. Stir the remaining 1½ cups of water into the bowl. If you like, add a tablespoon or two more of sugar.

3 Refrigerate the agua fresca for at least 1 hour to chill.

WATERMELON AGUA FRESCA

MAKES 6 CUPS

1 seedless watermelon (about 9 pounds), cubed

Splash of water

2–4 tablespoons sugar, if needed

1 In a blender, place the cubed watermelon and a splash of water. Pulse until pureed and very smooth. Give it a taste and add the sugar accordingly. If it's the beginning of summer, you may need to add a bit of sugar, but toward the end of the season your watermelon will be super sweet and will need none at all.

2 Pour the mixture through a strainer and into a pitcher, pressing the watermelon pulp with the back of a spoon to release any extra juices.

3 Transfer to the fridge to chill for at least 1 hour.

AGUA DE JAMAICA

MAKES 4 CUPS

½ cup sugar

¼ vanilla bean, scraped

5½ cups water, divided

½ cup dried hibiscus flowers + a few more for garnish

Juice from ½ orange

1 stick cinnamon

Ice cubes

Orange slices or lime wedges

1 In a small bowl, using your hands, mix together the sugar and vanilla bean caviar (the black beans scraped from the inside of the vanilla bean pod), making sure the vanilla is evenly distributed. Add the vanilla bean sugar and 4 cups of the water to a saucepan set over medium heat, and heat until the sugar has dissolved and the water is simmering. Remove from the heat.

2 Stir in the ½ cup of hibiscus flowers, orange juice, and cinnamon stick. Cover the pan and allow the tea to steep for 15 to 20 minutes, or until the mixture turns a deep maroon color.

3 Run the tea through a strainer and into a pitcher. Discard the tea leaf mixture and transfer the concentrate to the refrigerator to cool.

4 When ready to serve, mix in 1½ cups water to dilute. (Note: I personally like this drink slightly diluted, but if you don't, then simply don't add the extra water.) Pour over ice and garnish with a few hibiscus flowers and orange slices or lime wedges.

GO ON AN ADVENTURE WITH YOUR DOG

You probably don't have a dog that herds sheep. And you might not even have a dog. Heck, you might be a cat person! Basically, I just wanted to brag about Amelia's natural abilities, as any mother would. I do, however, believe in seeking out new adventures with your animal (or kids, use your kids!). There's something about newness that feels so right: It's revitalizing, refreshing, even magical.

I stumbled upon urban dog herding (this is apparently its technical term) from a blog reader after venting about Amelia's seemingly never-ending rambunctiousness. She kindly explained that Amelia wasn't doing what corgis are bred to do—herd sheep! It made complete sense to me, so I did some research and found a somewhat local farm in Malibu that offered classes for herding dogs. The idea behind urban dog herding is that it indulges dogs' natural abilities, challenges them, and gives them a great deal of exercise. I honestly didn't know what to expect. Would Amelia know what to do? Would she hurt the sheep? Would she be scared and run away? The minute she entered the pen and spotted the sheep, her natural instincts kicked in and she began running after them, grouping them together, barking orders— herding them!

Do

"SO HANGRY" KITCHEN BANNER

*For every 10 inspirational quotes, there are about 9 that make me roll my eyes. Usually they're cheesy, taken out of context, and just plain emo. Instead, I like the words around me to have a bit of humor, sass, or reflect how I'm feeling. In this case, it's all about **hanger** (hunger + anger), which is perfect because this banner lives in my kitchen. While there are a lot of banners online that have cute sayings and quotes, I found them to be surprisingly expensive, and I didn't always love what they were preaching. Luckily, making your own means you can add whatever saying you like and the supplies total only around $10.*

SUPPLIES

1 rectangle (18" x 14½") wool fabric

Ruler

Scissors

White or black iron-on letters

Piece of cloth

Iron

18" wooden dowel (see note below)

Fabric glue

Suede twine

Note: I could only find a wooden dowel that measured 26 inches long, so I trimmed mine with my sharp pruning shears.

1 Start by cutting the pointed bottom in the banner. Place the wool rectangle on your work surface vertically. Make a mark at the center of the bottom edge of the rectangle. Take a ruler and measure 5" from the bottom and make 2 marks, one on each side. To cut the point in the banner, cut from the bottom mark up to each side mark.

2 Position the letters on the banner, making sure they're straight. Use a ruler as a guide, if needed. Place a piece of cloth on top of the letters and iron them for about 2 minutes, being sure to keep an even amount of heat and pressure. Flip the banner over and iron its opposite side for about 20 seconds.

3 Remove the top piece of cloth and peel the plastic off the letters. If any of the letters give you a hard time, place the cloth back on and iron them for an additional 30 seconds to 1 minute.

4 Place the dowel at the top and fold the fabric over. Place fabric glue all along the seam and secure it for about 1 minute, or until glued.

5 Wrap and tie the suede twine around each end of the stick and hang!

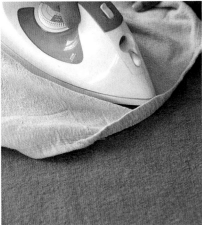

Live

RIDE YOUR BIKE TO A
NEVER-BEEN-BEFORE PLACE

I am obsessed with newness. And I don't mean a shiny new car, a new bag, or a new boyfriend. I mean fresh experiences. I wish I could fly to a country I've never been to before every few months, but that's usually not an option. Instead, I get on my bike and ride to a new part of town. Seeing new streets, new trees, and new places satisfies my curious mind. This one simple activity oftentimes leads to so many more adventures; it's inevitable that I'll come across a new-to-me restaurant I want to dine at or a new-to-me shop I want to dip into. While these memories are seemingly teeny next to larger life markers like graduating from college, landing a new job, or getting married, they're still pretty powerful.

Do

WATERCOLORED BURLAP-TEXTURED COASTERS

My friend, ceramicist Lindsay Emery from Suite One Studio, made many of the custom pieces you see in this book. My favorite pieces from her are ones where she presses a sheet of burlap onto the clay, creating a warm and beautiful texture. I wanted to attempt this technique, too, but since I'm not nearly as skilled as Lindsay (she works with porcelain) and I don't have a kiln in my garage, I used air-dry clay. These coasters couldn't be simpler to make. You cut out circles of clay, roll the burlap onto them, and wait for them to dry. I think the watercolors look beautiful in the impressions created by the burlap texturing, too.

SUPPLIES

Air-dry clay

Waxed paper

Rolling pin

Mason jar (or other large cylinder—to be used as a stencil)

X-ACTO knife

Bowl of water

2–3 sheets of burlap

Brush

Watercolor palette

1 Scoop out a mound of air-dry clay and place it in the center of a sheet of waxed paper. Using your rolling pin, roll the clay into a ¼" thickness. Place the Mason jar on the clay and use it as a guide to cut out your coasters with the knife.

2 To smooth out any rough edges, dip your finger into some water and rub the edges gently. Press a sheet of burlap onto the surface of the coaster, and remove it in one motion. Continue the process until you have made the desired amount of coasters. If your piece of burlap gets gunked up with clay, feel free to use a fresh sheet. Allow the coasters to dry on the waxed paper for at least 24 hours; depending on the weather, this may take up to 2 days.

3 When the coasters are dry, brush the tops with watercolor paint of your choice. I went with a cerulean blue. Really, you can't go wrong with any bright color. You might want to test out strokes on a piece of paper before applying them to the coasters.

HOMEMADE S'MORES KITS

I got the idea to make s'mores kits in berry baskets from the place where you go to find ideas about absolutely everything: Pinterest. The version I found didn't include anything homemade, which is just fine—I'm not judging! But as a believer that most things are better when they're homemade, I give you my version, involving homemade graham crackers and vanilla bean marshmallows. Choose the chocolate you like, fancy or good ol' Hershey's—either will work just fine. The graham crackers use cold butter to give you lots of layers, almost like the crust of a pie. And the marshmallows are light and fluffy with speckles of vanilla bean that make my eyes turn heart-shaped.

HOMEMADE GRAHAM CRACKERS

Graham crackers hold so many summer memories for me and, I'm guessing, for all of us. I think of being a kid and swimming all day. I think of sunburns and mosquito bites. I think of curling up in a sleeping bag (in my living room—I was big on living room camping!) and watching The Sandlot, *even though we had all seen it at least 10 times. I think of being under the star-filled night sky with the fire crackling and all of us kids assembling our s'mores with great excitement. I think of a time when my mind was filled with the thrill and anticipation of everything to come.* **MAKES 26**

1½ cups whole wheat flour + additional for working

1 cup all-purpose flour

¾ teaspoon salt

1 teaspoon baking soda

¼ teaspoon ground cinnamon

½ cup unsalted butter, cold

½ cup packed brown sugar

¼ cup granulated sugar

3 tablespoons good-quality honey

3 tablespoons milk

1 In a medium bowl, whisk together the 1½ cups of whole wheat flour, all-purpose flour, salt, baking soda, and cinnamon.

2 Using a box grater, grate the butter into the bowl of an electric mixer fitted with a paddle attachment. Add the sugars, honey, and milk. Mix on medium speed for 2 to 3 minutes, or until pale and fluffy, scraping down the sides of the bowl as needed. Reduce the speed to low, add the flour mixture, and mix until combined.

3 Turn out the dough onto a floured surface and divide it in half. Wrap each half in plastic wrap and transfer to the refrigerator to rest for 1 hour.

4 Remove the first half of dough from the refrigerator and roll it out between 2 pieces of parchment paper to a thickness of ⅛". Cut the sheet of dough into 3" squares. Don't bother separating the squares—we'll do that later, when they're chilled. Transfer to a baking sheet and place in the freezer to chill for about 5 minutes. Repeat with the second half of the dough.

5 Preheat the oven to 350°F. Separate the graham crackers from one another, spacing them a few inches apart on the baking sheets to allow a bit of room for spreading. Transfer the crackers back to the freezer for 15 more minutes, or until very hard. Bake for 10 to 12 minutes, or until the edges are lightly golden brown. Allow to cool on the baking sheets on a rack.

HOMEMADE MARSHMALLOWS

A lot of people who are really into cooking love to say everything is easy, but that's just not the case. The truth is some things are difficult to make at home, like candy. Kinda complicated. And croissants. Not worth it at all, in my opinion. But marshmallows could not be simpler, and the payoff is hu-u-u-ge. Homemade marshmallows are as different from the store-bought variety as night and day. These delightful puffy squares aren't too sweet, they're perfectly fluffy, and the vanilla bean flecks make me swoon. **MAKES 13 TO 16**

¼ cup confectioners' sugar

¼ cup cornstarch

¾ cup cold water, divided

2 envelopes powdered gelatin (from an 8-ounce package)

1½ cups granulated sugar

1 cup light corn syrup

½ teaspoon salt

1 vanilla bean, scraped, or 2 teaspoons pure vanilla extract

1   Before you begin making the marshmallows, let's do some much-needed prep. Sift together the confectioners' sugar and cornstarch onto a large plate. Next, coat an 8" or 9" square baking dish with vegetable oil. Sift a few tablespoons of the confectioners' sugar mixture into the baking dish and spread it around so the sides are dusted, too.

2   Pour ½ cup of the water into the bowl of a stand mixer with the whisk attachment. Sprinkle the gelatin on top and allow to sit for 10 minutes.

3   Meanwhile, in a medium saucepan with a candy thermometer attached, combine the granulated sugar, corn syrup, salt, and remaining ¼ cup of water. Heat the mixture over medium heat until the sugar has dissolved. Turn the heat up to medium-high and bring the mixture to a hard boil. Cook for 1 minute, or until the candy thermometer reaches 240°F.

4   Lower the whisk attachment and turn the mixer on low. Carefully add the boiling liquid to the gelatin mixture. Turn the mixer to high and beat for 10 minutes or until the mixture holds stiff peaks and the outside of the bowl is cool to the touch. Add the vanilla bean or extract. Beat for an additional minute or so until incorporated.

5   Pour the marshmallow into the prepared baking dish, smoothing out the top—it'll be sticky! Dust the top with 2 tablespoons of the confectioners' sugar mixture. Cover lightly with foil or plastic wrap and allow to set about 4 hours or overnight.

6 Run a knife around the dish edges and invert the marshmallow sheet onto a large cutting board, smacking the bottom of the dish. You may need to use your fingers to loosen the marshmallow sheet from the dish and gently slide it onto the cutting board. Using a sharp knife, cut the marshmallows into 2" cubes. You should get 13 to 16 marshmallows, depending on the pan you use. Toss the cubed marshmallows with the remaining confectioners' sugar mixture. Store the marshmallows in an airtight container for up to 1 week.

Tips: I purchased my very inexpensive Collins glasses from CB2. They have a good variety of glassware that is perfect for crafting. Armour Etch can be found at craft supply stores.

Do

GEOMETRIC-ETCHED COCKTAIL GLASSES

In the summer months, I want a few things: air-conditioning, a pair of cute sunglasses, half days on Fridays . . . and a cold cocktail in my hand whenever possible. These geometric-etched Collins glasses fit the bill. They're pretty, easy to craft-up, and look even better when filled with an ice-cold gin and tonic.

SUPPLIES

Scissors

Painter's tape

2 inexpensive Collins glasses

Rubber gloves

1 bottle Armour Etch

1 sponge paintbrush

Newspaper or craft paper

1 Cut out small triangles of painter's tape and apply them firmly in a random pattern on your glasses. After you're done, go back and make sure there are no bubbles in the tape. Super smooth is what you're going for!

2 Put on a pair of gloves to protect your hands. With the cap on, shake the Armour Etch. To hold the glass, I found it easiest to place my hand inside the glass and rotate it as I applied the etching paste. Open the bottle and dip your sponge paintbrush into the etching paste. Apply the etching paste in even strokes all over the glasses, leaving the bottoms of the glasses paste free. Place the glasses on a sheet of old newspaper or craft paper and allow to dry for about 5 minutes.

3 Remove the tape from each of the glasses. Wash with soap and water, using a soft sponge, before using.

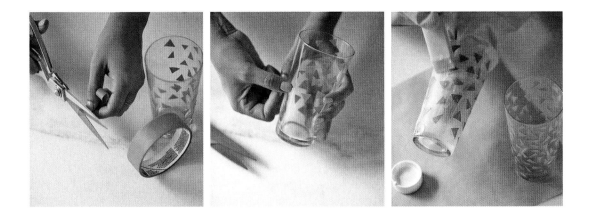

TRY A NEW SPORT

Years ago, when I was in a rut, I took a surfing class on a whim. I had never surfed in my life. I was afraid of the frigid water temperatures. (Have I told you that my ears are not keen on cold temperatures?) But I went and, even though, like most people, I didn't stand up on my first day, I survived, I learned, and I felt strangely accomplished. While I haven't been back (the cold water really is not my steez), I learned that trying a new sport can be invigorating and stimulating, and I've been inspired to try new sports and activities like dance classes, Pilates, long-distance cycling, and circuit training.

Summer

JULY

Salted Pretzel
Ice Cream

Matcha
Ice Cream

Sweet Corn
Ice Cream with
Blueberry Swirl

ICE CREAMS

My favorite summer days were spent in the South during college when I had nowhere to be and nothing to do. The dog days of summer were sultry, humid, and lazy. If you're lucky enough to be gifted a day in the summer with an open agenda, and an ice-cream maker, I recommend churning ice cream. All of these recipes use a good base and are adjusted to embrace the added flavors: matcha, pretzels, corn, and fresh fruit. I don't like picking favorites because I don't want to insult one of the flavors (they're sensitive!), but if I had to choose, its name pretty much rhymes with schmalted schnitzel.

SPECIAL EQUIPMENT FOR MAKING ICE CREAM

Mesh sieve

Ice-cream maker

Digital thermometer

Freezer-safe quart-size containers

Note: Each recipe requires you to chill the custard for at least 4 hours. If you don't want to wait, no biggie! I have a solution. Add about 1 teaspoon salt to a freshly prepared ice bath. Secure the bowl housing the custard right on top of the ice bath and transfer the whole thing to the fridge. Stick a thermometer in the custard and chill until it reads 40°F. This should take about 30 to 40 minutes. Once it reaches 40°F, it's ready to churn!

(continued)

SALTED PRETZEL ICE CREAM

Soaking crunchy pretzels in the milk turns ordinary plain ice cream into something unexpectedly magical. It almost makes you crave a side of mustard, but then you realize mustard and ice cream would be really strange. We're all weird, but not that weird.

MAKES 1½ PINTS

1¾ cups whole milk

30 small salted pretzels

4 egg yolks, at room temperature

⅔ cup sugar

1 cup heavy cream, at room temperature

1 Pour the milk into a large bowl and add the pretzels. Give it a good stir, making sure the pretzels have all been coated in milk. Cover the bowl with plastic wrap and transfer to the fridge to steep for 1½ hours. You'll know it's ready when the pretzels are softened and the milk smells just like them!

2 Run the milk through a strainer and into another bowl; press the pretzels with the back of a wooden spoon so they can release any milk. You will end up with about 1¼ cups of pretzel milk. Discard the pretzels.

3 Prepare an ice bath by adding a heaping handful of ice cubes to a large bowl and topping it off with a few splashes of cold water. Set a slightly smaller bowl inside it and place a sieve or strainer in it.

(continued)

4 In a medium bowl, whisk the egg yolks with the sugar until the mixture turns smooth and pale yellow. Add the pretzel milk to a medium saucepan. Turn the heat to medium and stir until the milk is hot to the touch, or until a digital thermometer reads 110°F. Whisking the entire time, add about ¼ cup hot milk (you can eyeball this measurement) to the beaten egg yolks. Pour the egg yolk and milk mixture into the medium saucepan and lower the heat to medium-low. Cook the mixture, stirring constantly, until a digital thermometer reads 170°F to 175°F and the custard appears thick and coats the back of a spoon.

5 Pour the custard through the sieve in the ice bath. Stir in the heavy cream until completely incorporated. Keep mixing until the mixture is room temperature. Place plastic wrap on the surface of the custard, which will prevent the formation of a skin, and transfer to the fridge for 4 to 5 hours, or until very cold.

6 When the custard is cold, churn it in the bowl of your ice-cream maker, according to the maker's instructions. Serve the ice cream right away for soft serve or transfer to a 1-quart container and freeze until firm, about 8 hours.

SWEET CORN ICE CREAM
WITH BLUEBERRY SWIRL

Corn and blueberries is an unexpectedly delicious union. The sweet corn and tart blueberries work wonders with each other. I urge you to give it a whirl . . . or in this case, a swirl.

MAKES 1½ PINTS

ICE CREAM BASE

1½ cups whole milk

1 ear corn, kernels sliced off and cob cut into chunks

¼ teaspoon salt

4 large egg yolks

¾ cup sugar

1 cup heavy cream

SWIRL

½ cup blueberries

2 tablespoons sugar

¼ cup heavy cream

Pinch of salt

Juice from ½ lime

1 *To make the ice cream base:* In a medium saucepan, add the milk, corn kernels and cob, and salt. Turn the heat to medium and cook until lightly simmering. Immediately turn off the heat and cover the pan. Allow to steep for 1 hour.

2 Pour the corn milk through a strainer and into a bowl, pressing the kernels with the back of a wooden spoon so they can release any excess milk. Discard the corn kernels and cob.

3 Prepare an ice bath by adding a heaping handful of ice cubes to a large bowl and topping it off with a few splashes of cold water. Set a slightly smaller bowl inside the larger bowl and place a sieve or strainer in it.

4 In a medium bowl, whisk the egg yolks with the sugar until the mixture turns smooth and pale yellow. Pour the corn milk into a medium saucepan. Turn the heat to medium and stir until the milk is hot to the touch, or until a digital thermometer reads 110°F. Whisking the entire time, add about ¼ cup hot milk (you can eyeball this measurement) to the beaten egg yolks. Pour the egg yolk and milk mixture into the medium saucepan and lower the heat to medium-low. Cook the mixture, stirring constantly, until a digital thermometer reads 170°F to 175°F and the custard appears thick and coats the back of a spoon.

(continued)

5 Pour the custard through the sieve in the ice bath. Stir in the heavy cream until completely incorporated. Keep mixing until the mixture is room temperature. Place plastic wrap on the surface of the custard, which will prevent the formation of a skin, and transfer to the fridge for 4 to 5 hours, or until very cold.

6 *To make the swirl:* Meanwhile, in a small saucepan set over medium-low heat, add the blueberries, sugar, heavy cream, salt, and lime juice. Cook for a few minutes, until the blueberries soften. Using the back of a spoon, smash the blueberries and cook until the mixture has turned a cohesive bright purple. Run the mixture through a strainer into a bowl, and discard the pulp. You should end up with about 3 tablespoons of blueberry sauce.

7 When the custard is cold, churn it in the bowl of your ice-cream maker, according to the maker's instructions. Transfer one-third of the ice cream to a 1-quart container and drizzle one-third of the blueberry sauce over it. Repeat layering with the remaining ice cream and blueberry swirl. Serve immediately for soft serve or freeze until firm, about 8 hours.

MATCHA ICE CREAM

This ice cream is about enjoying flavors from typically cooler months when it's hot and sweltering outside. Matcha green tea powder, with its earthy, slightly bitter notes, is perfect when combined with sweet cream. Sprinkle the ice cream with a little bit of black sesame seeds for some texture and pretty contrasting colors. **MAKES 1½ PINTS**

4 large egg yolks

¾ cup sugar

1¼ cups whole milk

¼ teaspoon salt

1 tablespoon matcha green tea powder

1 cup heavy cream

Black sesame seeds (optional)

1 Prepare an ice bath by adding a heaping handful of ice cubes to a large bowl and topping it off with a few splashes of cold water. Set a slightly smaller bowl inside the larger bowl and place a sieve or strainer in it.

2 In a medium bowl, whisk the egg yolks with the sugar until the mixture turns smooth and pale yellow.

3 In a medium saucepan, pour in the milk and add the salt. Turn the heat to medium and stir until the milk is hot to the touch, or until a digital thermometer reads 110°F. Whisking the entire time, add about ¼ cup hot milk (you can eyeball this measurement) to the beaten egg yolks. Pour the egg yolk and milk mixture into the medium saucepan and lower the heat to medium-low. Cook the mixture, stirring constantly, until a digital thermometer reads 170°F to 175°F and the custard appears thick and coats the back of a spoon.

(continued)

4 Pour about ¼ cup (you can eyeball this) of the custard mixture into a small bowl. Pour the rest of the custard through the sieve in the ice bath. Add the matcha powder to the reserved bowl of custard and whisk vigorously until the matcha has dissolved. (Little bits of matcha are okay.) Pour the matcha custard through the sieve and stir in the heavy cream until completely incorporated. Keep mixing until the mixture is room temperature. Place plastic wrap on the surface of the custard, which will prevent the formation of a skin, and transfer to the fridge for 4 to 5 hours, or until very cold.

5 When the custard is cold, churn it in the bowl of your ice-cream maker, according to the maker's instructions. Serve immediately for soft serve or transfer to a 1-quart container and freeze until firm, about 8 hours. You can sprinkle with the sesame seeds if you wish.

Do

PET TEEPEE

Amelia loves sleeping underneath things. She likes hiding under the couch, burrowing in freshly laundered sheets, and napping under my favorite throw. I'll admit, she's a bit of a weirdo. Even though she likes to bury herself, I wasn't sure how she'd take to this teepee. But the second I put it up, she knew it was for her. I watched with motherly pride as she went right into it, plopped down, and took a nap. If you build it, they will come!

SUPPLIES

5 (48") wooden rods

Paintbrush

Acrylic paint, color of choice

1 thick rubber band

Scissors

Suede rope (or twine)

Painter's canvas

X-ACTO knife

Grommets

Grommet pliers

1 Start by painting the ends of the wooden rods. This is completely optional, but I think it adds a fun detail.

2 Gather the wooden rods and secure them with a rubber band. Make sure the opposite ends of the rods reach the floor and feel sturdy. Also, be sure one end of the teepee is larger than the others—this will be the "door."

3 Using some of the suede rope or twine, secure the rods together (and cover the rubber band), weaving between the rods. Make sure the rods feel super sturdy.

(continued)

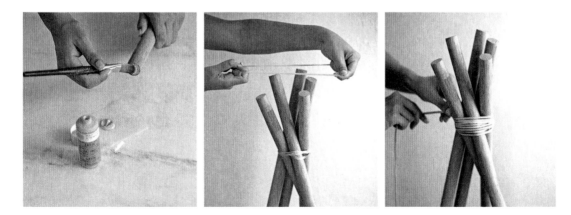

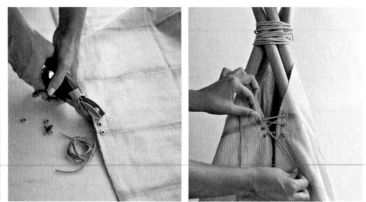

Note: For added pizzazz, I shibori-dyed my painter's canvas. For instructions, see pages 94–95.

4 Drape the canvas over the rods so you can figure out where the grommets will go. Make a small hole with an X-ACTO knife, and push the grommets through the hole. Place the washer piece on the opposite side of the fabric. Take the grommet pliers and sandwich the two together. This will secure the grommet completely. Repeat until you've made two or three more grommets.

5 Finally, thread suede rope through the grommets. Fold open the front flaps of the teepee. Proceed to place snacks or other dog or cat toys inside the teepee to persuade your pet that this is a chill place to be.

MAKE A TIME CAPSULE

I made a time capsule when I was in second grade, full of all of the things I loved at the time. I don't remember what was in it exactly, but I'm pretty sure there was a note about how much I loved my dog (I'm the same me), a Paula Abdul cassette tape, a packet of strawberry-flavored Fun Dip, and a few pink barrettes. I would do just about anything to get that time capsule back. Unfortunately, it was buried in the backyard of my old house, which has now been turned into a development of McMansions. I decided it was time to make a new one and stick a few meaningful-to-me things in it and hide it in the back of my closet for safekeeping. Here are some tips I followed.

1 Set a date when you're going to open the time capsule. I selected 2042. I'm hoping I'll have grandkids by then. Maybe it'll be something we'll do together.

2 Think about a safe storage place. If you know your family will never sell the house, then bury it in the backyard. Or opt for an attic or shelf hidden away. You can always take it with you when you move—you just can't open it!

3 Write yourself a letter: "Dear Adrianna in her fifties . . . " Tell your future self everything that's important to you, everything you're worried about, everything you hope will happen. I imagine my future self will tell me to calm down, stop worrying so much, and be hopeful.

4 Decide what to include in the time capsule. I like to include things that represent my interests, the time in which we live, and what's important to me, such as a ring I like, a picture of Amelia, a photo of Josh and me, an ice cream scoop, and random and cute tchotchkes.

5 Pick the container carefully. Are you burying it in the ground? Make sure it's a waterproof container. Are you storing it in your house or the attic? Make sure it's securely closed with a latch so you don't open it by mistake. Feel free to wrap that sucker in wrapping paper and label it.

BUILD A MEZZE PLATTER

Do you ever want to eat just appetizers for dinner? This is how I feel the majority of the summer. I want to graze like an elegant gazelle on a bunch of dips (though if you've ever seen me eat, you know I'm not as graceful). This mezze plate fits perfectly into my summer dinner plans; it is colorful and eye-catching and surprisingly filling enough to eat as a meal or ideal for serving as a first course. Each dip is different, but all work harmoniously with one another.

Mahamarrah is a Syrian dish that is rich, nutty, slightly sweet, and a little smoky. This hummus is classic. I like to shuck half of the chickpeas and leave the rest intact; the result is a hummus that is mostly smooth with just a bite of texture. Hourie, my friend and consultant on this mezze plate, said I somehow managed to make a non-ugly version of baba ghanoush. I was flattered! The speck of Italian parsley folded in helps give it a much-needed pop of color.

MAHAMARRAH (RED PEPPER–WALNUT DIP)

MAKES 1½ CUPS

3 red bell peppers

2 cloves garlic

Juice from ½ lemon

3 tablespoons good-quality olive oil

1 teaspoon pomegranate molasses

¼ teaspoon ground cumin

¼ teaspoon red-pepper flakes

3 tablespoons plain bread crumbs

3 tablespoons finely chopped walnuts

1 teaspoon salt

1 Preheat the oven to 400°F. Line a baking sheet with parchment paper. Place the whole peppers on their sides on the grates of 2 or 3 stove burners. Turn the flames to medium-high and char the skins; using a pair of tongs, turn the peppers every 30 seconds or so until the skins are blackened, about 2 to 3 minutes. If you have an electric stove, you can actually place the peppers directly onto the coils.

2 Transfer the peppers to the baking sheet and roast for 20 minutes, or until the peppers have softened. Allow the peppers to sit just long enough so that they're cool enough to handle. Using a knife, scrape off the charred skins, cut off the tops, and discard the seeds and ribs.

3 Pulse the garlic in a food processor until minced. Next, add the roasted peppers, lemon juice, oil, molasses, cumin, red-pepper flakes, bread crumbs, walnuts, and salt. Pulse until very smooth, about 1 minute. Transfer the mahamarrah to a serving bowl. Alternatively, you can make this dip up to 3 days ahead and store it in the refrigerator. Allow the dip to come to room temperature before serving. If water has risen to the top of the dip, not to worry—simply mix in an additional tablespoon or two of bread crumbs.

TABBOULEH SALAD

MAKES 1½ CUPS

¼ cup superfine bulgur (see note)

1 tablespoon olive oil

Salt

Juice from 3 lemons, divided

1 small bunch Italian parsley, finely chopped (about ½ cup)

5–6 mint leaves, finely chopped (about 2 tablespoons)

1 Persian cucumber, cut into small cubes

10 cherry tomatoes, quartered

1   In a medium bowl, mix together the bulgur, oil, a pinch of salt, and the juice from 2 of the lemons. Allow the bulgur to marinate for about 5 minutes. During this time, the acid from the lemon will cause the bulgur to bloom.

2   To the bulgur, add the parsley, mint, cucumber, tomatoes, and ½ teaspoon of salt. Give it a taste, and if you'd like it a tad bit more tart, squeeze in the juice from the remaining lemon. Adjust the salt according to taste.

Note: If you don't have access to superfine bulgur, you can use fine bulgur. To do this, add ¼ cup of fine bulgur, ½ cup of water, and a pinch of salt to a small saucepan. Set it over medium heat and bring the water to a simmer. Cook until the water has evaporated and the bulgur has bloomed.

BABA GHANOUSH

1 eggplant (about 1 pound)

1 clove garlic, minced

¼ cup good-quality olive oil

Juice from ½ lemon

½ teaspoon salt + additional if needed

Pinch of ground cumin

1 tablespoon finely chopped flat-leaf parsley

1 Preheat the oven to 400°F. Line a baking sheet with parchment paper. Using a knife, score the eggplant a few times. Place the whole eggplant on its side right on the grates of a gas stove burner. Turn the flame to medium-high and char the skin, turning the eggplant, until the skin is blackened, about 4 to 6 minutes. If you have an electric stove, you can actually place the eggplant directly onto the coils.

2 Transfer the eggplant to the baking sheet and carefully slice it in half. Roast the halves, cut side up, for 20 minutes, or until the eggplant is very soft. Allow the eggplant to rest until cool enough to handle.

3 Scoop the eggplant flesh into a bowl and discard the skin. Add the garlic, oil, lemon juice, ½ teaspoon salt, and cumin. Whisk the mixture together until smooth. Fold in the parsley and adjust the salt according to taste.

CLASSIC HUMMUS

MAKES 1½ CUPS

1 can (16 ounces) chickpeas, strained, ¼ cup liquid reserved

1 clove garlic

Juice from ½ lemon

1 tablespoon tahini

½ teaspoon salt + additional if needed

1 tablespoon good-quality olive oil

Ground sumac

1 In a food processor, pulse ½ cup of the chickpeas until coarsely chopped. Transfer to a small bowl.

2 The remaining chickpeas should measure out to be 1 cup. Squeeze each chickpea between your thumb and index finger and pop it out of its skin. Discard the skins. Repeat this process until you've shucked all of the chickpeas. This usually takes me about 7 to 10 minutes.

3 In a food processor, pulse the garlic until minced. Add the shucked chickpeas, the reserved chickpea liquid, lemon juice, tahini, and ½ teaspoon salt. Pulse until very smooth, scraping down the sides every so often. Add the reserved coarsely chopped chickpeas and pulse for about 15 seconds, or just until combined. Adjust the salt to your liking.

4 Transfer to a clean serving bowl, make "swoops" in the top of the hummus with a butter knife, and drizzle with the oil and a few dashes of sumac.

Do

ROOM SPRAY

Have you ever entered someone's house and it smells just like them? The smell isn't bad; it's just very distinctive and recognizable. When I was a kid, I was in love with homes that smelled like laundry day. It made them feel warm and clean and made me want to curl up on the couch with a book. This room spray smells just like a ball of warm clothes tumbling in the dryer.

SUPPLIES

1 (12-ounce) spray bottle

1 cup filtered water

4 tablespoons vodka

4 drops lily of the valley essential oil

2 drops lavender essential oil

3 drops lime essential oil

Note: I found all of these essential oils at my local health food store.

1 To the spray bottle, add the water and vodka.

2 Next, drop in each of the essential oils; give it a whiff and adjust the smell according to your liking.

3 Screw on the top and give the spray bottle a light shake. Spray the mixture a few times in each room for that deliciously fresh smell. This spray will last up to 3 months.

Note: Anthropologie's sale section and Target are good places to find pretty spray bottles.

BEER CAN POLLO A LA BRASA

Make

Being a first-generation American with Peruvian and Colombian parents is interesting. I don't exactly feel 100 percent American, but it's also difficult for me to identify with the countries of my parents. For years I felt awkward about this strange limbo, but now I simply embrace it by coming to terms with the fact that I'm a bit of both and that's okay. This beer can chicken is a symbol of that understanding, in the form of a tasty, juicy chicken! On the one hand it's very American—who else would put cheap beer up a chicken's bottom—and on the other it is very Peruvian, imbued with the flavors of my childhood. Pollo a la Brasa is a very popular style of Peruvian rotisserie chicken. It is usually cooked over a fire using ingredients nearly impossible to find in the States: aji amarillo and black mint. But when you crave the taste of your childhood, you make do with ingredients you can find, so in place of the aji amarillo, I use Fresno chiles or jalapeños, and I opt for plain ol' mint. The beer imparts flavor and tenderness. You can cook this either on a grill or in the oven; both will work wonderfully. MAKES 4 SERVINGS

½" knob peeled fresh ginger

2 cloves garlic

1 tablespoon soy sauce

1 tablespoon red wine vinegar

1 tablespoon finely chopped fresh mint

½ Fresno or jalapeño chile pepper

1½ teaspoons ground cumin

1½ teaspoons kosher salt

1 teaspoon freshly cracked black pepper

½ teaspoon sweet paprika

1 fryer chicken (about 3½ pounds)

1 can (12 ounces) lager beer

1 In a food processor, pulse the ginger, garlic, soy sauce, vinegar, mint, chile pepper, cumin, salt, black pepper, and paprika until the mixture resembles a paste.

2 To prep the chicken, discard the bag of innards and pat it dry with paper towels. Transfer the chicken to a large bowl. Separate the chicken's skin from its breast. You might need a sharp knife to get the process started; after that, you should be able to simply pull it away from the breast with a bit of force. Rub the marinade under the skin, in the cavity of the bird, and on top of the skin. Cover the bowl with plastic wrap and transfer to the refrigerator to marinate for at least 4 hours, or ideally overnight.

3 Open the can of beer and pour about one-quarter of the beer into a glass (feel free to drink it!). Fit the chicken onto the open can so the chicken sits upright (you may need a friend to help you keep the can of beer steady). Give her a name. Mine was named Lindsay.

(continued)

4 *If you are making this on the grill:* Prepare your grill for indirect heat. If you're using a charcoal grill, pour the coals to one side of the grill, leaving the opposite side free of coals. If you're using a gas grill, turn on only one-half of the burners.

5 Transfer the chicken to the cool side of the grill, using the legs and can of beer as a support system to keep the chicken upright. Shut the grill lid and cook the chicken for about 50 minutes. At that time, insert a meat thermometer into the thickest part of the thigh—if it reads 160°F, the chicken is completely cooked. If it needs more time, be sure to check on it in 5-minute increments.

6 *If you are making this in the oven:* Put a rack in the lower third of the oven and preheat the oven to 350°F. Line a baking sheet with parchment paper or a silicone mat. Transfer the chicken/beer can contraption to the center of the baking sheet, so the chicken is standing upright. Roast for about 1 hour, or until the chicken's skin is golden brown and a thermometer inserted into the thickest part of the thigh reads 165°F.

7 Transfer the chicken with the help of tongs, and possibly a friend, to a cutting board or large plate. Allow it to cool slightly before you try to remove the can of beer. The chicken will be hot! The beer will be hot! Oven mitts work very well in this case, though they will get dirty, so beware. Help from a friend is a must! Remove the beer can from the chicken and allow the chicken to rest on the cutting board for 10 minutes before cutting it up to serve.

VISIT A THRIFT STORE

Thrifting makes me giddy. I'm always on the hunt for props for the blog. For years, I strictly stuck to eBay because thrift stores and their clutter overwhelmed me. I slowly eased into it and now consider myself a bit of a pro. Over the years I've learned some tips that have helped me uncover treasures amongst tons of junk at thrift stores.

1   Have an idea of what you're looking for. Is it clothes? Tchotchkes? Furniture? Kitchen goods? I try to narrow down my categories. This helps when I'm greeted with rows and rows of stuff.

2   Go on the day that new inventory is put out. Most stores have a set day. It's oftentimes a Tuesday, after they've scoured their resources for goods. Go on that day!

3   If you're in the market for clothes, come dressed for the part. Most thrift stores don't have dressing rooms, so this means leggings and a fitted T-shirt are your best bet for slipping clothes over your head and getting an honest fit.

4   Examine goods before you buy them. My mother does this even with new things she buys, and it's a really good idea. Look for discoloration, chips, nicks, and brand markings.

5   Haggle. Some stores do not allow this. Ask! Simply say, "Are these prices negotiable?" If they are, then I usually open with, "Would you take (insert price here) for this?" I try to say it in as decisive and confident a manner as possible. And I don't say it with a smile. I mean business!

6   Pay attention to the season. For instance, in Palm Springs, where I do most of my thrifting, the best discounts are during summertime because that's when the most tourists come. I save my dollars and spend the most in the summer because of the amazing discounts I'm able to score.

A⁵ AMERICAN VINTAGE

Make
SHRUBS

Have you ever had a shrub? It's an old-school thing, English, I believe; they're deliciously tart and really effervescent. The fruit and sugar macerate together for a few days and ferment in a slow and natural way—think kombucha-esque! After a few days, the syrup is strained and vinegar of choice is added. I did some of the work for you and paired the syrups and vinegars that I think work best. The applications are really fun. The syrups work in sparkling water, cocktails, and my favorite, snow cones. **MAKES ABOUT 3 CUPS EACH**

PEACH SHRUB

2 cups finely chopped peaches (about 2 peaches)

2 cups sugar

½ cup (4 fluid ounces) champagne vinegar

CHERRY SHRUB

2 cups finely chopped cherries (about 1 pound)

2 cups sugar

1 cup (8 fluid ounces) balsamic vinegar

STRAWBERRY SHRUB

2 cups finely chopped strawberries (about 2 pints)

2 cups sugar

½ cup (4 fluid ounces) sherry vinegar

1 In a 4-cup Mason jar (or other jar with an airtight lid), place the chopped fruit and sugar. Using a long wooden spoon, stir the fruit and sugar together, smashing the fruit against the side of the jar. Cover the jar with its airtight lid and allow to stand on the kitchen counter, in indirect sunlight, for about 72 hours, shaking it every so often. You might notice that the sugar gathers at the very bottom; if this happens, just give the jar a shake.

2 On the third day, pour the syrup through a strainer into a clean jar, pressing the fruit and any residual sugar with the back of a wooden spoon. Discard the fruit chunks and any leftover sugar. Stir in the recommended vinegar and secure with a lid. Place in the fridge until you're ready to use. Shrubs are usually okay when used within 6 months. If the shrub shows any signs of mold or cloudiness, discard.

(continued)

SOMETHING SIMPLE:
SHRUB SPARKLER

Lots of ice

6 tablespoons (3 fluid ounces) strawberry or peach shrub or ¼ cup (2 fluid ounces) cherry shrub

¾ cup (6 fluid ounces) sparkling water

In a glass filled with ice, stir together the shrub and the sparkling water.

SOMETHING BOOZY:
PEACH BOURBON COCKTAIL

2 tablespoons (1 fluid ounce) peach shrub

2 tablespoons (1 fluid ounce) bourbon

Lots of ice

Splash of cava or champagne

Add the shrub, bourbon, and ice to a glass. Mix until very cold. Top with a splash of your favorite cava or champagne.

SOMETHING BOOZY:
STRAWBERRY SHRUB
GIN AND TONIC

2 tablespoons (1 fluid ounce) strawberry shrub

¼ cup (2 fluid ounces) gin

Lots of ice

6 tablespoons (3 fluid ounces) tonic water

In a glass, mix together the strawberry shrub, gin, and ice until very cold. Top with the tonic water and mix one more time.

SOMETHING FUN:
SHRUB SNOW CONES!

¼ cup (2 fluid ounces) shrub

Crushed ice

Transfer the shrub to a bottle with a spout. Fill a glass with crushed ice and pour the shrub over it.

Shrub Sparkler

Strawberry Shrub
Gin and Tonic

Peach Bourbon
Cocktail

Shrub Snow
Cones!

Do

CELERY-STAMPED FARMERS' MARKET BAG

I'm going to admit something to you: I'm not one of those people who look beautiful when they go to the farmers' market. There are no scenes of me with perfectly groomed hair, sniffing fragrant ripe fruit. Instead, I wake up super early, throw on some jeans and a T-shirt and sunglasses to cover my tired eyes, and grab a coffee on my way there. Let's just say I rely on my bag to deliver most of the cuteness. This bag is stamped with vegetables—celery, to be exact. The blue bag is Breton-inspired, while the green takes its color from, well, celery. Feel free to get creative with the pattern, too!

SUPPLIES

1 rib celery

Foam brush

Fabric paint

Plain canvas bag

1 Evenly trim the top of the rib of celery, the leafy end. (Keep in mind that celery ribs tend to be smaller on top and larger near the stem; I found that I liked the smaller shape near the top.)

2 Dip your foam brush in a bit of fabric paint and apply a light coat to the exposed celery end. Firmly press the celery onto the canvas bag in any pattern you like. Reapply paint as needed.

3 Lay flat to air-dry for 2 to 3 hours.

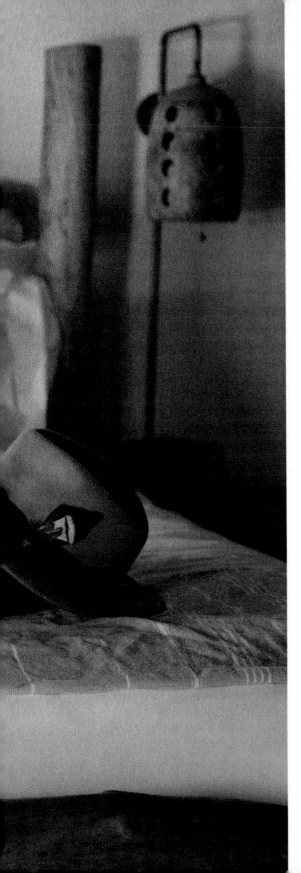

HAVE A STAYCATION

There are summers when going on vacation isn't in the cards. Whether it's due to budget woes or simply lack of time, sometimes staycations are all I'm going to get. To enjoy them properly, I follow a set of rules: no cleaning, no errands, and no cooking. Sticking to these guidelines helps push me out the door to enjoy my city just like a visitor would. Here are some activities I partake in while on a staycation.

1 Stay in a hotel. If I have the extra funds, I love staying in a hotel. Nothing beats waking up in a new part of town, in a new bed, with room service on its way.

2 Visit a museum. I don't go to museums every weekend, but whenever I do go, it feels like such a treat.

3 Do something obnoxiously touristy—in my case, taking pictures in front of the Hollywood sign or going on a Hollywood tour bus.

4 Go to the beach. I don't live near the water, so sitting outside near the ocean always feels a bit like a vacation.

5 See music in an outdoor venue. Summer shows at the Hollywood Bowl with a picnic are pretty dreamy.

PERUVIAN CEVICHE

There are a lot of styles of ceviche, a Central and South American raw seafood dish. Ceviche from Baja, Mexico, is crazy different from the ceviche that Colombians in Cartagena eat. And the ceviche that Peruvians eat is wildly distinctive from both. My mother is from Peru, so I grew up eating a rendition similar to the one you see pictured. Even now, as an adult, having eaten tons of different types of ceviche, this particular one feels like home. Traditional Peruvian ceviche uses aji amarillos. Since they're nearly impossible to find outside of Peru, I like using a red Fresno chile. And, just as a bonus, it gives the leche de tigre *(the dish's citrusy marinade) a gorgeous pink hue.* MAKES 4 APPETIZER SERVINGS

2 cloves garlic, trimmed

½ rib celery, coarsely chopped

1" knob peeled fresh ginger, sliced

½ Fresno chile pepper, coarsely chopped

¼ red onion, coarsely chopped + 1 cup vertically slivered red onion

¾ cup lime juice (from about 5 limes)

¼ teaspoon fine-grain sea salt + additional to taste

½ pound sea bass

Handful of fresh cilantro leaves

1 large sweet potato, boiled and chopped

½ cup canchas

1 In a food processor, pulse the garlic, celery, ginger, chile pepper, and one-quarter red onion until finely chopped. Add the lime juice and ¼ teaspoon salt. Pulse once more until completely combined. Give it a taste, and if you like, add a few pinches of salt. You have just made leche de tigre (tiger's milk)!

2 Prepare the fish by rinsing it under cold water. Pat the fish dry with paper towels and transfer it to a cutting board. Cut the fish into 1" cubes and place them in a bowl. Sprinkle the fish with a few pinches of salt. Pour the leche de tigre over the fish. Toss until completely coated. Transfer to the refrigerator to chill for 10 to 15 minutes. During this time, the acid will "cook" the fish.

3 Divide the fish among 4 plates. Garnish each mound of ceviche with a few slivers of red onion, a few cilantro leaves, some chopped sweet potato, and a handful of canchas.

Note: Canchas are a large-kerneled corn often eaten as a snack. You can usually find them at Latin supermarkets. You can also grab a small bag of corn nuts from the market—they're the same thing!

Do

ACTIVATED CHARCOAL
BROWN SUGAR SCRUB

Most people use scrubs in the winter, when the dry, cold air leaves skin dull and chapped. But, since I live in California, I find that my skin needs some scrubbing during hot, dry summer months. I recently jumped onto the activated charcoal bandwagon after having used the sticks to purify my drinking water. This DIY combines many things you might already have in your medicine cabinet. The result is a scrub that is cool and unique enough to give away to friends but awesome enough to use in your own shower over and over again.

SUPPLIES

1 cup light or dark brown sugar

4 (280 mg) capsules of activated charcoal

2½ tablespoons jojoba oil

8 drops of lavender essential oil (or other fragrant essential oils)

1   To a medium bowl, add the brown sugar. If you can, open the capsules and pour in the activated charcoal. If you're having trouble twisting the capsules open, you can snip the end with a pair of scissors. After you pour in the charcoal, add the jojoba oil and essential oils.

2   Mix all of the ingredients together, being sure to really get in there and rub the mixture with the sugar. If you like, feel free to put on a pair of latex gloves (the activated charcoal gets under your nails!). Divide among 3 or 4 containers. The scrub will last, in an airtight container, for up to 3 months.

Note: You can find the activated charcoal capsules online or in any vitamin store.

Note: Feel free to use other oils like olive oil, avocado oil, or walnut oil. All are great for your skin!

SEPTEMBER

HEIRLOOM TOMATO MARINARA SAUCE

I believe in buying the rejects at the farmers' markets. Heirlooms are crazy expensive most of the time, but not in September. Many stands have a bin full of "seconds." It's when they sell their bruised, too-ripe heirloom tomatoes for more than half off. Don't let looks fool you; the best heirloom tomatoes for this sauce will be a little wrinkly, might leak a bit, and will defy the idea of a perfectly round tomato—really, the uglier the better! I take advantage of this time and make all the salsa and marinara sauce I can manage. This tomato sauce recipe is inspired by my mama. She never makes marinara sauce from a can, but instead opts for fresh tomatoes. It's simplicity at its finest. MAKES 2 SERVINGS

2½ pounds heirloom tomatoes

1½ tablespoons olive oil

3 cloves garlic, minced

1 small shallot, finely chopped

Pinch of red-pepper flakes

¼ teaspoon dried oregano

½ teaspoon salt or to taste

1 tablespoon finely chopped basil (about 3 or 4 leaves)

1   Fill a medium saucepan with water and bring it to a boil over medium-high heat. Using a knife, score the bottoms of the tomatoes, making an X. Carefully plunge the tomatoes into the hot water for about a minute (this time may vary depending on how ripe your tomatoes are), or until the skins begin to shrivel up a bit. Remove the tomatoes from the water and allow them to cool slightly, about 3 minutes. Peel the tomatoes and discard the skins.

2   Just a heads-up: This process is a bit messy, but it's worth it! Squeeze out the tomato seeds and set them aside on your cutting board. Transfer the tomato flesh to a bowl. Place a sieve on top of the bowl and add the seeds and any excess juice that may be on the cutting board to the sieve. Press the seeds to release the juice that usually coats them—that's the good stuff! Repeat until you've worked your way through all of the tomatoes.

(continued)

3 In a medium saucepan (you can use the one you used to boil the tomatoes—just be sure to empty it), heat the oil over medium-low heat. Cook the garlic and shallot until softened, about 2 minutes. Add the tomatoes and juice, red-pepper flakes, and oregano. Bring to a slight simmer and cook on low for about 15 to 20 minutes, stirring every so often, or until the sauce has thickened. Some tomatoes are saltier than others, so I say salt to taste. I needed about ½ teaspoon of salt. Stir in the basil. You can serve the sauce right away on top of a bed of pasta, or you can transfer it to a glass container and save it for later. Tomato sauce stored in an airtight container in the fridge will last up to 3 days.

FLAVORED HONEYS

At the tail end of September, we get small signs that the weather is about to change. The last of the tomatoes make an appearance at the market; fresh corn slowly fades; the light begins to shift to the more autumnal yellow that I love so much; and my in-box fills up with promotions for fall clothes. Maybe I'm stretching the truth a bit by saying we have a real autumn in Los Angeles. We do not. We just have hints it's coming, which is (almost) good enough for me. I like to do a few things to anticipate the new season, mainly because autumn is my favorite season of them all. I like to break out the flannel sheets. (It usually ends up being way too early, but

(continued)

I'm an overzealous person by nature.) I like to stock up on teas. And I love making infused honeys. Rosemary, with its wintry and savory notes, is such a complement to sweet and floral honey. The hot honey is inspired by the spicy honey I love at the Brooklyn pizza joint Paulie Gee's. And the vanilla bean honey is so satisfying in a mug of warm tea.

A tip about what type of honey to use: I love varying varieties of honey, but since I'm infusing it with ingredients, I like to use a moderate-quality and relatively mild-flavored honey like mesquite or clover. I leave the fancy stuff—i.e., my beloved wildflower, avocado, or buckwheat—to enjoy alone.

ROSEMARY HONEY
¾ cup honey
1 sprig fresh rosemary

VANILLA BEAN HONEY
¾ cup honey
½ vanilla bean, scraped

HOT HONEY
¾ cup honey
¼ teaspoon red-pepper flakes

In a small saucepan set over medium-low heat, add the honey. When the honey is hot (this doesn't take long), mix in the rosemary, vanilla bean and caviar, or red-pepper flakes. Immediately transfer the flavored honey to a glass jar. Allow to cool to room temperature. When cooled, remove the ingredient that's infusing (the rosemary or vanilla bean). Strain the honey into another jar. Label the jar, seal it with an airtight lid, and transfer to the refrigerator to keep for up to 3 weeks.

GO ON A LONG HIKE

I like to go on long hikes and channel my inner Bear Grylls. Let me step back and say that the hiking terrain around Los Angeles is no Mount Everest, but I still like to pretend I'm climbing a huge mountain. What I pack in my backpack varies, depending on how long I intend to be out. Many of these things are mainstays and will help me if I get in any sticky situations.

1 Nut bars. These are light and small and pack a huge punch in terms of calories, flavor, and sustenance.

2 Water. Duh. Obvious advice alert! While I love my glass water bottles, I prefer plastic ones when hiking—less weight!

3 Silicone collapsible dog bowl. It saves space, it's lightweight, and it can be used as a food or water bowl for Amelia.

4 A fully charged smartphone. This is one part potential rescue tool, one part camera.

5 Long-sleeve shirt. Depending on when you're hiking and where, the weather can change unexpectedly.

6 Small flashlight. I never hike at night. There are ghosts and coyotes and I hate the dark, but just in case, I always bring a small light source with me.

7 Small trash bags. Is there a greater offense than littering? Maybe murder. Maybe. I always make sure to clean up after myself.

8 A mini first aid kit. I've never used it, but I always pack one.

9 A notebook. I may sound a bit lofty right now, so please bear with me. I'm most inspired by nature, by the way the sun peeks through the trees, the way the breeze feels, the way the trees smell. It makes me feel all the feelings. I like taking a break to jot down thoughts and ideas.

Do

PUT UP A GALLERY WALL

I'm the furthest thing from an interior designer, but that doesn't mean I don't want my home to feel as beautiful and warm as possible. I've always been drawn to gallery walls; something about the organized chaos satisfies my eyeballs in the best way. Unfortunately, they can go wrong very quickly because they're actually quite hard! Here are some tips I've found helpful.

1 Keep the frames the same color and style. I prefer clean white frames (hello, IKEA!) with some light wood mixed in.

2 Hang the largest painting off-center. My friend Lara gifted me the largest one you see pictured here. It's definitely the main focus, but instead of putting it in the center, which would be the obvious choice, I think it pleases the eye to hang it off-center and to the right.

3 Remember that color is important. Make sure there aren't too many colors that clash. And equally disperse the color across the wall. I like to bring in a few solid-colored images to break up the color.

4 Make sure to have a range of sizes. I've found that one big photo or print, a couple midsize ones, and a few small frames work best.

5 Mix and match the types of art. I like to have a variety of watercolor paintings, photographs, line drawings, and acrylic paintings.

6 Make sure you have a large enough collection to fill the entire wall. Collections oftentimes grow slowly—not to worry! Rather than buying just to buy, choose your pieces carefully. If you don't have that many frames in the beginning, start your gallery on a smaller wall. The fun is in the process of watching it grow.

CRISPY BAKED SPICY CHICKEN WINGS

If I'm ever in a terrible mood, the cure is always a plateful of chicken wings. I know that might come as a bit of a surprise; the obvious guess would be a cup of hot chocolate or slice of pie, but I just really love wings. I love every variety and ethnicity. Korean chicken wings? My all-time favorite. Deep-fried and southern? Cue: heart-eyed emoji. The range of chicken wings I like is wide, but one thing they must be is crispy. Since heating up a big pot of oil for frying never sounds like too much fun, I depend on the baking powder trick. The result is oven-baked chicken wings with the perfect amount of crunch and crispness. Serve them with cold beer and sticks of celery and blue cheese dressing, and, if you like, you can turn on that game people tend to love so much. **MAKES 3 TO 4 SERVINGS**

WINGS

2 pounds small chicken wings and/or drummettes

1 teaspoon baking powder

BLUE CHEESE DRESSING

¼ cup buttermilk, shaken

3 tablespoons sour cream

1 tablespoon blue cheese crumbles

Salt

SAUCE

½ cup hot-pepper sauce (such as Frank's RedHot)

¼ teaspoon Worcestershire sauce

¼ teaspoon garlic powder

¼ teaspoon ground red pepper (optional)

2 tablespoons unsalted butter

1 *To make the wings:* Pat the chicken wings and drummettes dry using paper towels. Transfer them to a cooling rack set over a baking sheet. Sprinkle both sides of the chicken with the baking powder. Place the chicken in the refrigerator, uncovered, to chill for at least 6 hours or up to overnight.

2 Preheat the oven to 450°F. Line a baking sheet with parchment paper. Place the chicken on the baking sheet and bake for 20 minutes. Turn and cook for an additional 10 to 15 minutes, or until the chicken skins are crispy and golden brown.

3 *To make the blue cheese dressing:* While the chicken is cooking, make the dressing. In a small bowl, whisk together the buttermilk, sour cream, and blue cheese crumbles. Add a few pinches of salt, according to taste.

4 *To make the sauce:* In a medium saucepan set over medium heat, add the hot-pepper sauce, Worcestershire, garlic powder, and red pepper, if using. Bring the sauce to a light simmer and cook for about 5 minutes, or until the sauce is reduced by half. Turn off the heat and stir in the butter.

5 Place the cooked wings and drummettes in a large bowl. Pour the sauce on top and cover the bowl with a plate. Shake the bowl so each piece of chicken is thoroughly coated.

6 Serve the wings with the blue cheese dressing on the side.

Live

START A NEW HOBBY

I've been throwing ceramics for a little more than a year. It was the first hobby I ever picked up, though I had wanted to start one for as long as I can remember. I was craving an outlet that wasn't associated with cooking or my job. I wanted to create something with no real pressure, no expectation that it had to be good. It is freeing: sitting on a stool and throwing plates and bowls. It is meditative. I think, I don't think, I listen to podcasts, I gossip with my friend Lara, and I connect with people I otherwise wouldn't have connected with. Here are some tips about starting a new hobby.

1　Choose the hobby. This is the hardest part. A good place to start is to think back on all the activities you enjoyed as a child. Also, cost may come into play since some hobbies can be pricey. Search and keep searching until you find something you want to try.

2　Take a class. The easiest way to dive into a new hobby is to take a class. This was important to me because I wanted to learn the basics of ceramics; also, classes oftentimes offer equipment you otherwise wouldn't want to buy. And taking a class means there is no cleanup in your home to deal with.

3　Be okay with not being good. I'm a very competitive person, so I struggle with this every time I go to ceramics class. I constantly have to keep my frustration at not being an amazing ceramicist in check.

4　Stick with it. The better you get at something, the more fun it is. This takes time. Patience is key.

5　Make friends. When you walk into a room where everyone is doing the same activity, you immediately share a common interest. It makes it so much easier to meet new acquaintances and make friends.

FANCY-ASS PB&JS

One of my more popular columns on the blog is my "Fancy-Ass" series. It's where I take something normal, usually from our childhoods, and make it super freaking fancy. I took a leap at the opportunity to make you all a Fancy-Ass PB&J. There's no better month to do this than September, when Concord grapes are at their peak. Here's how you do it: You make your own Concord jam. It'll be runnier than the jelly you probably grew up with, but it's so much better. Make your own peanut butter. It couldn't be easier. And, of course, if you don't have the time, feel free to buy some. And lastly, get a good loaf of bread. I recommend brioche. The results are sublime and will make your inner 6-year-old giddy. MAKES ENOUGH FOR 10 SANDWICHES

CONCORD JAM

1 pound Concord grapes, picked off the vine

1 cup sugar, divided

¼ teaspoon salt

Juice from ½ lemon

HOMEMADE PEANUT BUTTER

2½ cups (12 ounces) shelled and skinned roasted peanuts

½ teaspoon salt

1–2 tablespoons peanut oil or coconut oil (heated slightly until runny)

1 loaf of your favorite bread (I used brioche, but I bet challah or a Pullman loaf would be delicious)

1   *To make the jam:* Peel the skins off of the grapes. This is a bit mundane, so play some music or put on your favorite TV show! Add the skins to a food processor, along with ½ cup of the sugar. Blend until pureed.

2   In a medium saucepan set over medium heat, add the pureed skin mixture, grape flesh, remaining ½ cup sugar, salt, and lemon juice. Bring to a slight simmer, then turn the heat down to medium-low. Cook for 15 to 20 minutes, or until the grapes have softened. Using the back of a spoon, smash the grapes, being careful because they'll splatter! Run the mixture through a sieve into a bowl and discard the pulp and seeds. Transfer back to the saucepan and cook until the mixture reaches 220°F on a digital thermometer. (I know many people rely on the cold plate test, but with Concord grape jam, I find it easiest to just cook it to this temperature.)

3   Immediately pour the jam into a jar. It will be slightly runnier than the Concord grape jelly you might be accustomed to—it's supposed to be that way! And it will definitely thicken as it cools.

4 ***To make the peanut butter:*** In a food processor, puree the roasted peanuts and salt for 1 minute, then scrape down the sides of the bowl. Continue processing until the peanuts turn from ground to pastelike. Slowly drizzle in the oil and continue pureeing until smooth, about 5 minutes. Place the peanut butter in an airtight container and store it in the refrigerator.

ACKNOWLEDGMENTS

To Danielle Svetcov, my agent, my counsel, and friend: Thank you so much for guiding and believing in me. This project absolutely would not exist if it weren't for you pushing me and it forward. Thank you a thousand times.

To my editor and friend (and second mother to Amelia should anything ever happen to me), Dervla Kelly: Thank you for the passion, creativity, enthusiasm, encouragement, and ideas you've put into this book. I'm grateful to you always. A big thank-you to the designer of this book, Rae Ann Spitzenberger, for making it so much prettier than it was in my head. To Yelena Nesbit, thank you for your work and excitement, and for appreciating s'mores pop tarts as much as I do. A special hug and thank-you to Mollie Thomas, Hope Clarke, and Aly Mostel. And to the rest of the team at Rodale: I'm honored to be working with you all.

Billy Green, the Brandi to my Kim, the Ramona to my turtle time, the Nene to my "bye girl": Thank you for your work on this book. Your spirit made everything from recipe testing to baking and shooting pies during a wretched heat wave actually fun—that is a talent!

To Hourie Sahakian: I'm so grateful to have a friend who is as baking-obsessed as I am. Thank you for letting me bounce ideas off of you, taste-testing stuff, and giving me the best feedback ever.

A big hug to ceramicist Lindsay Emery for being ridiculously generous by spending weeks making custom pieces for this book—thank you, thank you!

To a number of friends who have helped shape this book in one way or another: Samantha Kuntz, Michael Weiss, Natalie Lewis, Samantha Duenas, Priti Patel, Jason Stewart, Cassie Tregellas, Lara Meyerratken, Whitney Adams, Sean Weiss, and Tre Knight.

Thank you to my parents, German and Tatiana, who by example have taught me what passion, hard work, and determination look like. And to my brother, Daniel, for thinking everything I make is magical; you're the best.

To my love, Joshua: Thank you for being the best taste-tester, recipe tester, and critic. Riding through life with you feels like a gift.

To Amelia: You can't read or hold up a book, so this is actually sort of pointless, but know that you make my life better. You make me stop and appreciate the smallest nuances in life. Thank you for all the unconditional love you give so freely.

And lastly, to the readers of *A Cozy Kitchen,* I somehow managed to make a whole career out of putting free recipes on the Internet. I definitely could not have done that without you. Thank you for being as obsessed with pie as I am, thank you for making my recipes, thank you for visiting and telling me about your lives, thank you for being you. I'm forever grateful to have your support.

SHOPPING SOURCES

Many of the plates, glasses, and supplies I used to make the crafts in this book have been sourced from the places below. They are some of my favorite stores, and they're where you can find what you need to create anything you see in this book.

MICHAELS CRAFT STORE

michaels.com

Did you know you can buy craft supplies online from Michaels? They have a wide selection of supplies, everything from acrylic paint to wooden dowels.

AMAZON

amazon.com

You can buy many of the craft supplies in this book directly from Amazon. If you have Amazon Prime, even better.

MARTHA STEWART CRAFTING SUPPLIES

shop.marthastewart.com

It's no surprise that Martha Stewart, queen of all things home related, would have a killer crafting line. I usually buy her products, like acrylic paints (she really does have the best colors), at Michaels, but you can buy them directly from her if you like.

THE SPICE STATION

spicestationsilverlake.com

My neighborhood spice store has a wide variety of spices. What I love most about this store is that I have the option to buy more exotic, new-to-me spices in smaller quantities. This means I get to try all sorts of spices without having to commit to a large jar. And, luckily for you, they ship!

SUITE ONE STUDIO

suiteonestudio.com

Ceramicist Lindsay Emery made many of the custom pieces you see in this book. All of her work is made entirely by hand, topped with beautiful, homemade glazes. Her pieces make mealtime that much more enjoyable.

SCHOOLHOUSE ELECTRIC & SUPPLY CO.

schoolhouseelectric.com

For all things home related, my go-to is Schoolhouse Electric & Supply Co. My bedding, trays, and various tchotchkes are oftentimes from this store.

MICHAEL LEVINE FABRIC STORE

lowpricefabric.com

Hands down, the best fabric store in all of Los Angeles. And, luckily for all of us, they have an online store. Order linen for the Shibori Tie-Dyed Table Runner (page 94) or rose-hued wool (it's the softest) for the "So Hangry" Kitchen Banner (page 174).

ORIGINAL LOS ANGELES FLOWER MARKET

originallaflowermarket.com

If you live in the Los Angeles area, the LA Flower Market is your best bet for finding really beautiful florals at an affordable price. If you don't live in Los Angeles, keep in mind that most large cities have their own flower market; seek it out! Trust me, it'll be worth it.

TERRAIN

shopterrain.com

Many of my favorite linens, mugs, and throws come from Terrain. Their style is usually rustic and cozy, which are both right up my alley.

IKEA

IKEA.com

It takes a lot of mental preparation to get me to go to IKEA, but the inexpensive prices (and frozen yogurt) are worth the trip. I often find things that are perfect to hack. Examples: Hand-Painted Pillow (page 112) and Doormat with a Message (page 88).

WORLD MARKET

worldmarket.com

I love to head to World Market for everything from kitchen essentials to spices. And if you ever go during the holidays, you'll find they have some of the most adorable decorations.

ANTHROPOLOGIE

anthropologie.com

Everyone's favorite store for all things cute and pretty. Many of my kitchen and tabletop goods are from their sale bins.

HEATH CERAMICS

heathceramics.com

Their matte ceramics are beautiful and come in a variety of colors. Their plates make food look beautiful, their vases make flowers pop, and their mugs are the perfect vessel for coffee or tea.

CB2

cb2.com

CB2 is the mecca for affordable furniture and tabletop goods. They make my favorite set of glasses, called the Marta. Their low price points and sleek and modern designs make me swoon.

INDEX

Boldface references indicate photographs.

THE COZY SQUAD

AMELIA
Author's Muse

BILLY GREEN
*Assistant/Photography/
Emotional Support*

JOSHUA PRESSMAN
*Taste-Tester/Recipe Tester/
Fun Boyfriend*

**DANIELLE
SVETCOV**
*Trusty
Literary
Agent*

DERVLA KELLY
*Senior Editor/
Boss Bitch*

MOLLIE THOMAS
Kick-Ass Assistant Editor

RAE ANN SPITZENBERGER
Designer/Font and Color Magician

**YELENA NESBIT
& ALY MOSTEL**
*Publicity Department's
Dynamic Duo*